HOLBEIN

IOANNES HOLPENIVS BA   SILEENSIS
SVI IPSIVS EFFIGIATOR   Æ XLV

HOLBEIN

JANE ROBERTS

BLOOMSBURY BOOKS
LONDON

(frontispiece)
Self-portrait

FLORENCE, Galleria degli Uffizi. 1543. Black and coloured chalks on pink prepared paper, extensively worked over in watercolour and gold paint. Inscribed: IOANNES HOLPENIVS BASILEENSIS SVI IPSIVS EFFIGIATOR AE. XLV.

The status of this drawing is problematical, for it has been extensively worked over by later hands. The features of the artist are the same as those seen in the miniature self-portraits of the same date (Plate 91), but while Holbein's hair is shown in the drawing it is covered with a hat in the miniatures. The inscription is not original but apparently follows the wording of an old one which is still partly visible. It is possible that in its original state this drawing was used as a preparatory study for the miniatures: the technique is, in any case, very similar to that of Holbein's drawings of the second English period. Much of the overpainting was apparently carried out at the start of the eighteenth century when the drawing was incorporated in the collection of artists' self-portraits formed by Cardinal Leopoldo de' Medici; at the same time it was enlarged on all four sides.

ACKNOWLEDGEMENTS

First published in Great Britain in 1979 by
Oresko Books, 167 Hermitage Road, London N4 1LZ

Copyright © Oresko Books Ltd

This edition published 1988 by
Bloomsbury Books an imprint of
Godfrey Cave Associates Limited
42 Bloomsbury Street, London WC1B 3QJ
under license from Minotaur Publishing Co Ltd

ISBN 1 870630 661

Printed in Yugoslavia

HANS HOLBEIN THE YOUNGER

HANS HOLBEIN'S BIOGRAPHERS are confronted with a number of problems. There is a tantalizing scarcity of documentary evidence concerning the artist's life, and while there is a superabundance of works, in particular portraits, to fit into his life history, many of his most important works are known through written descriptions, preparatory studies and copies alone. This is true both of his early works, including all the house façades, and some of the later ones such as *The More Family Group* (see Plate 29) and the Whitehall mural (see fig. 9). In addition, Holbein reached stylistic maturity early and died, in his mid-forties, without crucially altering his style for at least the last fifteen years of his life, so that it is often difficult to place his undated works.

The barest skeleton of his biography is well known. He was born in Augsburg in 1497/98, the second son of the painter Hans Holbein who gave him his earliest training. The eldest son of the family, Ambrosius, was also an artist and for a time the two brothers shared a studio. They are seen together with their father as onlookers in a panel from the elder Hans's *Baptism of St. Paul* (fig. 1). By 1515 the two younger Holbeins had moved from their native town and country and settled in Basel, where Hans was principally based until 1526. The brothers visited Lucerne in 1517 and 1519, and from there they most probably travelled to Italy. Hans the younger became a member of the painters' guild in Basel in 1519 and in the same year took over his brother's studio; after this date nothing further is heard of Ambrosius so we must presume that he died around this time. In the following year, 1520, Hans was elected chamber master of his guild and became a citizen of Basel. Also about this time he married Elsbeth Schmid, a tanner's widow with one son; in the ensuing years the couple produced two boys, both of whom became goldsmiths, and two girls (see Plate IV), and while Holbein journeyed to Antwerp and to England his family appears to have lived permanently in Basel. Meanwhile Hans Holbein the elder continued to paint until the time of his death in 1524, finding work throughout the larger towns of southern Germany. He apparently left a quantity of valuable painting materials at Isenheim, which his second son attempted, unsuccessfully, to retrieve on numerous occasions after his father's death.

There are dated works by the younger Holbeins throughout their residence in Basel, including panel paintings, mural decorations and designs for book illustrations. In 1523–24 Hans travelled through France and the Netherlands (see Plates 27 and 28), and two years later he left Basel for the first of his two visits to England. The reason for this visit is suggested in a passage concerning the artist in a letter of 29 August 1526 addressed by Erasmus, another resident of Basel, to his fellow-scholar Aegidius in Antwerp: 'Hic frigent artes, petit Angliam ut corrodat aliquot Angelatos.' ('Here the arts are freezing, [so Holbein] is on his way to England to pick up some angels [coins] there.') Carrying this letter and the introduction it contained Holbein visited Aegidius in Antwerp on his way to England. He had reached London by December 1526 and remained there until the summer of 1528. During this first visit he must principally have been occupied in painting *The More Family Group* (see Plate 29) and other miscellaneous portrait commissions. There is no certain evidence that he had any direct contact with the royal court at this time, and in 1528 he returned to Basel, where he bought a large house overlooking the Rhine; in 1531 he acquired the adjoining house as well. However, by the early 1530s, the religious and political climate in Basel was, if anything, even less encouraging for artists than it had been in 1526 and Holbein therefore set out for England for a second time, once again stopping at Antwerp on the way. By July 1532 he had arrived in London and dated works punctuate his residence there until his sudden death of the plague in 1543. In 1538 and 1539 he was travelling on the continent with the principal object of recording the likenesses of prospective brides for King Henry VIII, and for a short period at this time he visited Basel, where his family was still residing. There a banquet was held in his honour and the City Council offered him a pension and privileges to try to tempt him to remain permanently, but Holbein must by then have had too many commitments in London to make such a project possible. From 1536 at least, he had been working for the king and his private portait-painting practice in London was evidently thriving. In addition, he was apparently very happy there.

At the time of his death Holbein was a resident of the

fig. 1
Hans HOLBEIN the elder (c.1465–1524)
The Baptism of St. Paul
Augsburg, Städtische Kunstsammlungen.
c.1503–04. Oil on panel 187·8 × 90·7 cm.

This painting occupies part of the central
panel of the altarpiece entitled *The Basilica of
St. Paul*, painted c.1503–04 by the elder Holbein for the Convent of St. Catherine in
Augsburg. Among the onlookers at the baptis-
mal ceremony are the two Holbein sons, Ambrosius and Hans, with their father. The two
boys were also depicted together by their
father on a sheet of metalpoint studies dated
1511 in Berlin (Staatliche Museen, Kupferstichkabinett).

parish of St. Andrew Undershaft in the City of London,
and yet his will makes no mention of any property
owned by him there, beyond such immediate possessions as a horse and some clothing. He was never a
naturalized Englishman and his family continued to
reside in his substantial house in Basel, latterly thriving
on the proceeds of the will of a rich uncle and the
pension granted to Holbein by the City Council,
notwithstanding his failure to return home permanently. In London he left several debts and 'two chylder
wich be at nurse', who were evidently illegitimate and
who were to be provided for out of the proceeds from
the sale of his possessions. Neither his will nor any
contemporary document makes any mention of the
studio at Whitehall with which Holbein is always said

to have been provided by the king, but in view of his
extensive work for the court it is far more likely that his
studio was there than that it was adjacent to or part of
his house in the east of London.

We know almost nothing about Holbein's character,
although we may perhaps try to guess at it from one of
his self-portraits (frontispiece and Plate 91), three of
which are dated 1543, the year of his death. Although
his facial features do not suggest a fiery disposition
there is a story concerning his quick temper which has
been repeated often since it was first reported in print
by the Flemish painter Karel van Mander in *Het Leven
der Doorluchtighe Nederlandtsche en Hoogduytsche Schilders* of
1618. According to van Mander, when the artist was
painting the portrait of a certain lady for the king he
received an unannounced visit from a nobleman, and
dismissed his visitor by hurling him downstairs, before
rushing to the king to apologize.

From the evidence contained in Holbein's surviving
and recorded works we can form some idea of the social
circles in which the artist moved. Through his activity
in designing title-pages and book illustrations during
his years in Basel he met the printer Froben (Plate 12)
and the scholar Amerbach (Plate I) and thus became
acquainted with other humanists residing in that town
and, in particular, with Erasmus (Plates 24, 26 and
111), who, at that time, was employed by Froben;
around 1530 Holbein also painted the portrait of
Melanchthon (Plate 46), another member of this circle.
Several of Thomas More's writings were published in
Basel and were illustrated with designs (Plate 101)
provided by either Hans or Ambrosius Holbein, but it
seems that Hans Holbein and Thomas More did not
meet until the artist first travelled to England. They
must have struck up a close friendship, and it is
probable that Holbein was resident in More's house at
Chelsea for much of this first stay in England. It
appears then that Holbein portrayed these humanists
out of friendship and not merely as their paid portrait
painter; Erasmus was certainly an important source of
encouragement and influence for the artist's career.
Soon after Holbein's first arrival in England More
wrote in a letter to Erasmus dated 18 December 1526:
'Your painter, dearest Erasmus, is a wonderful artist,
but I fear he is not likely to find England so abundantly
fertile as he had hoped; although I will do what I can to
prevent his finding it quite barren.' Another scholar
with whom Holbein appears to have contracted a close
friendship was the French poet Nicolas Bourbon (Plate
81), for after Bourbon's return to France from England
in 1535 he included the artist among a list of those 'with
whom you know me connected by intercourse and
friendship', to be greeted 'in my name as heartily as you
can'. But in general we know little about the circles in
which Holbein moved during his second stay in
England. In the year of the artist's return, 1532, More

resigned from office and Archbishop Warham (Plate 36), with whom Holbein had also been in contact earlier, died. Holbein, therefore, had to find new friends and patrons, and he appears to have turned to the community of Hanseatic merchants resident in the German steelyard in the City of London. The first record of his return to London is, indeed, apparently contained in the date, 26 July 1532, on the portrait of a member of the German community, generally thought to be the goldsmith Hans of Antwerp (Plate 50). In any case, Hans of Antwerp must be listed among Holbein's friends, for he witnessed the artist's will and acted as one of his executors; his co-witnesses were other, lesser-known, members of the English artistic community with whom Holbein presumably passed much of his time.

Through his employment at the English court Holbein must have come to know most of the people of power and importance in the land. Owing to the fact that the relevant accounts for the years 1533 to 1537 are missing we do not know exactly when the artist entered royal employ, although from 1538 at least he was receiving an annual salary of £30 from the crown. In Bourbon's letter of 1536 Holbein is referred to as 'the royal painter', and it is possible that by this date he had been working for Henry VIII for at least a year as Thomas Cromwell, the King's Secretary, was portrayed by him in 1534 (Plate 61). Holbein was certainly well known to one of the royal servants, Sir Philip Hoby (Plate 82), for they travelled to Brussels together in 1538 to visit Christina of Denmark on the king's behalf. And the German, Nicolaus Kratzer, a royal astronomer, whom Holbein had portrayed in 1528 (Plate 41), employed the artist to carry Protestant books to Cromwell in 1536. It should be noted here that during his stay in Basel from 1528 to 1532 Holbein had affirmed his allegiance to the reformed religion and could therefore settle happily in England during the troubled years leading up to More's execution. His personal connection with the crown can only be guessed at on the basis of such paltry evidence as the fact that he was frequently paid his salary in advance and that, on New Year's Day 1540, Holbein presented the king with a portrait of Prince Edward, usually identified with the one now in Washington (Plate 73), while the painter was presented by the king with a gold cup on the same occasion.

Holbein's training in his father's studio in Augsburg provided him with a solid grounding in the techniques of oil painting, draughtsmanship and designing for books and the decorative arts as practised in Germany in the last years of the fifteenth century. Augsburg was probably the first south German town to feel the effects of the Italian Renaissance, for it stood on one of the main routes out of Italy to the north and was consequently a thriving commercial and intellectual

centre. A work such as *The Baptism of St. Paul* of c.1503–04 (fig. 1) by the elder Holbein reveals details of Italian influence only in a very limited way: both the composition and the perspective are disunited while the fall of drapery and the proportions of the figures are more typical of late mediaeval than of Renaissance art. Compared to this work the younger Holbein's *Flagellation of Christ* (Plate 2), painted approximately ten years later, and the *Christ in the Tomb* of 1521 (Plate 11) have a power and expressiveness worthy of Grünewald, achieved through an economy of gesture and setting which can be found throughout Holbein's *oeuvre*. What is probably Holbein's earliest dated work is the table-top which was painted to celebrate the marriage of Hans Baer in June 1515 and which is, therefore, the first evidence of the artist's presence in Basel (Plate 1). This curious object shows a wide variety of animals, birds and instruments, depicted as a rather crude *trompe-l'oeil* and surrounded by country scenes of revelry and jousting. Similar characteristically German types reappear in Holbein's design for the Haus zum Tanz (Plate 6) of about five years later and also in several of his woodcut designs of the 1520s. Other early works reveal more typically Italian features, such as the *all'antica* detail in the backgrounds of the 1516 portraits of Jakob Meyer and his wife (Plates 3 and 4) and in the decoration for Jakob von Hertenstein's house of 1517–19 (Plate 10), while Holbein's skill in pure penmanship can be seen in the marginal notes he added to a copy of the 1515–16 edition of Erasmus's *Encomium Moriae* (Plate 9). If the date of Holbein's birth, derived from an inscription on a portrait drawing by the elder Holbein of his two sons, is correct then he would have been only eighteen or nineteen years of age when this group of works was executed.

Holbein's talents as a decorator were soon put to great purpose on the façades of houses in both Lucerne and Basel. Much of his time during his periods of residence in Lucerne must have been spent in adorning both the interior and exterior of the new house of Jakob von Hertenstein, chief magistrate of Lucerne, on which building work had ceased only in 1517, the year of Holbein's first visit to the town. The house was demolished in 1825 but some of Holbein's designs survive (Plates 7 and 10), and we can reconstruct the appearance of the whole from the evidence provided by these drawings and by various written descriptions. In Basel Holbein decorated several houses, of which the best-known is probably the Haus zum Tanz of c.1520–22 (fig. 2 and Plates 5 and 6), belonging to the wealthy goldsmith Balthasar Angelrot. Once again the house has been demolished but its original appearance is known from drawings and written descriptions. In both cases, but especially in that of the Haus zum Tanz, there was a wealth of *all'antica* detail and sophisticated illusionism which must surely have derived from a

fig. 2
H. E. von BERLEPSCH
Reconstruction of the Haus zum Tanz Façade
Basel, Offentliche Kunstsammlung,
Kupferstichkabinett. 1878. Watercolour
62 × 91·5 cm.

This reconstruction was made on the basis of
written descriptions and earlier views of the
house at a time when it was still standing; the
Haus zum Tanz was demolished in 1907.
Holbein's work on the house, which belonged
to the goldsmith Balthasar Angelrot, can be
dated c.1520–22. It was his most daring ven-
ture in the exploitation of *trompe-l'oeil* techniques combined with detail which mostly
derived from Italian sources (see Plates 5 and
6).

firsthand knowledge of works by Mantegna (fig. 3) and
of the highly decorated polychrome exteriors of
contemporary north Italian churches such as the
Certosa at Pavia. In his designs for the Haus zum Tanz
Holbein apparently had to accommodate existing
window and door openings spaced at irregular intervals, and to overcome this he cloaked the whole in a
web of painted architecture with a sophistication far in
advance of other northern decorative schemes. This
fictive architecture was inhabited by a curious, and
typically German, mixture of dancing peasants, weird
animals and scenes from ancient history, including a
great horseman apparently leaping from the façade at
second-floor level, a conceit taken from a description by

Livy. It is hard, if not impossible, to imagine the effect
created by Holbein's paintings on the Haus zum Tanz.
The house stood at the corner of two narrow streets so
that the decoration could never have been seen easily
from ground level; the main façade was on the shorter
of the two sides. Nevertheless it was a *tour de force* for an
artist still in his early twenties and must have
established further his reputation in Basel.

At the same time as Holbein was at work on the Haus
zum Tanz, he also began a large decorative scheme
intended to cover the walls in the Great Council
Chamber of Basel Town Hall, which was rebuilt from
1508 to 1521. Fragments of his work, carried out in two
periods, from 1521 to 1522 and c.1530, still survive
(Plate 48), as do the artist's studies for the individual
scenes (Plates 8, 47 and 49). Once again there is a strong
Italian flavour to this series of scenes from ancient and
biblical history, intended to inspire the councillors in
their discussions. The painted architectural framework
in which the separate episodes were set reminds one
immediately of the religious and secular cycles of the
Italian Renaissance (fig. 4) and in particular of those in
the Palazzo Ducale and the various *scuole* in Venice.

The Triumph of Riches and *The Triumph of Poverty* which
the artist painted for the Guildhall of the German
steelyard in London c.1532–33 belong to a scheme of a
similar nature to that of the Basel murals and are also

fig. 3
Andrea MANTEGNA (c.1431–1506)
The Triumph of Caesar, canvas five: *Sacrificial
Bull and Elephants*
Hampton Court Palace, Royal Collection.
Tempera on canvas c.274 × 274 cm.

This canvas is one of a group of nine *Triumphs*
painted by Mantegna in the 1480s for the
Palazzo Ducale at Mantua. The series soon
became well-known through the publication of
engravings recording each scene, and pictorial
quotations from it appeared in paintings and
sculpture throughout Europe during the following decades. The triumphal procession in
the upper frieze of Holbein's façade of the von
Hertenstein house in Lucerne (see Plate 10)
was clearly connected with this series, as were
his two *Triumphs* for the German steelyard (see
fig. 5 and Plate 58), painted around fifteen
years later.

known only through copies (fig. 5) and preliminary
designs (Plate 58). Both their medium, tempera on
canvas, and their content recall Mantegna's *Triumph of
Caesar* series (fig. 3) which Holbein might have seen in
Mantua during his supposed Italian visit, although he
would probably have known the compositions well at
second hand through engravings. At this point it is
perhaps justifiable to consider the tiny composition of
Solomon and the Queen of Sheba (Plate 85), for although the
purpose of this painting is not known it shares various
features with the large-scale decorative works and is
comparable in many ways to the composition of
Rehoboam Rebuking the Elders from the Basel Great
Council Chamber (Plate 47). The miniature painting is
highly finished, and there are some exquisite passages,
particularly in the female figures at bottom left. Even

bearing in mind the different contexts, scale and degrees of finish of this painting and the preparatory studies for the two *Triumphs*, it is hard to believe that stylistically *Solomon and the Queen of Sheba* follows rather than precedes them, as has always been argued. In the absence of evidence to the contrary it should surely be dated right at the beginning of Holbein's second English period, c.1532.

The problematic dating of the *Solomon* miniature is symptomatic of Holbein's *oeuvre*, for apart from his very earliest works he progressed without any very clear stylistic development. Although there certainly appears to be a new sense of polish to the works of his second English period, we do not know how such works compared with the final appearance of *The More Family Group*, for instance, one of the oustanding achievements of his first English period. The problem is complicated by the fact that a large proportion of Holbein's work during the first part of his career has not survived. In Basel his main activity was the production of religious paintings, especially altarpieces, for the main churches of the town. These were nearly all destroyed during the waves of purging and persecution that swept through Switzerland during the Reformation of the 1520s and 1530s, and the fact that any religious works survive at all in Basel is chiefly due to the collecting activities of

fig. 4
General view of the Camera degli Sposi showing the west and north walls.
Mantua, Palazzo Ducale.

The frescoes painted by Mantegna in the Camera degli Sposi in the early 1470s contain numerous features which could possibly have served as models for Holbein's paintings on house façades and for his wall decorations in Basel Town Hall. Both the *all'antica* detail and the *trompe-l'oeil* effects of figures painted so as to appear to walk in front of or behind the painted architecture are prototypes of decorative schemes both in Italy and in the north of Europe. In addition, the court scene on the north wall, depicting members of the ruling Gonzaga dynasty, may be seen as a precedent for Holbein's *More Family Group* (see Plate 29).

the artist's friend and patron, Bonifacius Amerbach (Plate I), who formed the greater part of the collection of works by Holbein now preserved in the Offentliche Kunstsammlung in Basel. Amerbach collected chiefly small-scale religious works, and the altarpieces were in the main destroyed entirely. Among the few surviving large-scale religious compositions are the two altar-

fig. 5
Jan de BISSCHOP (1628–71)
Copy of Holbein's 'The Triumph of Poverty'
London, British Museum, Department of
Prints and Drawings. Pen and wash over black
chalk 34·5 × 47·4 cm.

This drawing provides evidence of the appearance of one of the two *Triumphs* which Holbein executed for the Guildhall of the German steelyard c.1532–33 (see Plate 58). The original compositions contained life-size figures and were painted on canvas; they rapidly became known throughout Europe, as is clear rom the large number of surviving copies, and greatly enhanced Holbein's reputation. The pictures remained in the precincts of the steelyard until 1598, when it was closed by Elizabeth I. Soon after they were presented to Henry, Prince of Wales, and were later in the collection of Thomas Howard, second Earl of Arundel. The last record of their existence is in 1666, when they belonged to the offices of the Hanseatic League in Paris, having been brought there from Flanders. It is probable that de Bisschop's copies of the two paintings were made in Amsterdam. In *The Triumph of Poverty* the aged and decrepit figure of Poverty sits on a waggon driven by Spes and drawn by two oxen called Negligentia and Pigritia and two asses called Stupiditas and Ignavia. These animals are led by four women, Moderatio, Diligentia, Solicitudo and Labor. Behind the waggon there are other figures such as Infortunium, Mendicitas and Miseria. The lesson to be learnt by the merchants from this composition was the virtue to be found in honest poverty. The programme for both pieces has been attributed to Sir Thomas More, and if this were so it would provide a unique piece of evidence of Holbein's continued contact during his second visit to England with the principal patron of his first visit.

pieces of the 1520s, *The Solothurn Madonna* of 1522 (Plate 13) and *The Meyer Madonna* of c.1528 (Plate VIII). In *The Solothurn Madonna* the Virgin and Child are seated between St. Nicholas and St. Ursus under a bare tunnel-vault, while in *The Meyer Madonna* they stand before a niche and in front of them there is a curious group containing the patron, Jakob Meyer, and his two wives, two sons and one daughter. Meyer's first wife had died in 1511 and his two sons both died in 1526. X-rays have revealed that the portrait of the first wife was added at the back, while those of the second wife (see also Plate 4) and of the daughter were altered, and it is possible that when Holbein left Basel in 1526 the painting was unfinished, and that he completed it, with alterations, after his return two years later. These altarpieces employ different Italian compositional types: in *The Solothurn Madonna* the *sacra conversazione*, in *The Meyer Madonna* the *Madonna della Misericordia*, both in distinctive quasi-Italian forms with semi-circular arches crowning the centre of each panel. We may presume that, following their Italian prototypes, the architecture within the paintings would have been complemented by that of the frame, particularly of *The Solothurn Madonna*. In both cases there is an important deviation from the Italian models in placing all the figures in the foreground rather than ranging them in depth, but in general these paintings, as with the decorative murals, are remarkably Italianate. We can even find Italian sources for the actual poses of the figures: the brilliant foreshortening of the Christ Child's outstretched arm must surely owe something to the similar gesture of the Virgin in Leonardo's *Virgin of the Rocks* (fig. 6), and the static grouping of the saints and Madonna and Child of *The Solothurn Madonna* must similarly have been modelled on north Italian altarpieces. Another religious work from this decade is the *Noli Me Tangere* in the Royal Collection (Plate II). In certain respects this panel appears old-fashioned when compared to the two altarpieces, and it certainly retains the power and Grünewald-like character of the early *Flagellation* (Plate 2) and *Christ in the Tomb* (Plate 11). But in other ways *Noli Me Tangere* is a more accomplished work. Sixteenth-century iconoclasts have deprived us of strictly comparable material, and this panel is therefore alone in Holbein's work in even attempting to portray a figure subject in a landscape setting. The colour throughout, and in particular of the scene within the rock, is of comparable intensity to that in the eight scenes of *The Passion Altarpiece* in Basel (Plates 19–21), which must also date from c.1524.

Holbein's stylistic development, such as it was, can most easily be traced through a study of his portraits, many of which are dated. Owing largely to historical accident and to the fact that there was little if any demand for religious art in Protestant England where Holbein spent almost half of his active life, he came to be known primarily as a portraitist even during his own lifetime. In the course of the correspondence concerning the portrait of *Christina of Denmark, Duchess of Milan* (Plate VII) the English ambassador in Brussels mentioned that Henry VIII esteemed Holbein chiefly as 'very excellent in making Physiognomies'. The companion portrait of *Jakob Meyer* and *Dorothea Kannengiesser*

fig. 6
LEONARDO da Vinci (1452–1519)
The Virgin of the Rocks
London, National Gallery. Oil on panel
189·5 × 120 cm.

This altarpiece, which was commissioned from
Leonardo in 1483 for the Church of San
Francesco Grande in Milan, was well known
and often copied during the sixteenth century.
It is possible that the gesture and foreshortening of the Virgin's hand inspired the very
similar gesture of the Christ Child in Holbein's
Meyer Madonna (Plate VIII). This connection,
coupled with the numerous other Italianate
features found in Holbein's work, suggests that
he travelled to north Italy early in his career.

portraits of 1516, for which there are preparatory
silverpoint studies in Basel, employ the sophisticated
device of placing both Meyer and his second wife
within the same arched loggia in which they are also
linked by their glances, although the panels on which
they are painted are quite separate. As in the case of *The
Solothurn Madonna* and *The Meyer Madonna*, the spatial
unity of the portrait pair would presumably originally
have been strengthened by details of the framing.
Another early portrait is that of Holbein's friend and
benefactor, *Bonifacius Amerbach*, dated 1519 (Plate I),
which reveals the direct influence of the art of Albrecht
Dürer both in the skilful concentration on facial
features and in the handling of the paint, as in, for
example, the older artist's portrait of *Oswald Krel* of
1499 (fig. 7). Holbein was over a generation younger
than Dürer, but in many ways their careers can be
considered in parallel: although Dürer was based
principally in his home town of Nuremberg, he paid
frequent visits to Augsburg and Basel and also to
Antwerp, and his style was greatly affected by his direct
contact with contemporary Italian art. In addition,
both Dürer and Holbein were close to Erasmus, who
described Dürer in a letter of 1525 as 'an artist of the
first rank', although three years later he wrote: 'Dürer
painted my portait, but it was nothing like.' Erasmus
apparent sat to Dürer in Antwerp in 1520 in the
presence of Nicolaus Kratzer (Plate 41); Dürer's
engraved portait of *Erasmus* of 1526 was probably made
on the basis of a sketch executed at this sitting.

Seven years after the portrait of *Amerbach*, Holbein
painted the curious pair of panels, *Laïs Corinthiaca*
(Plate III) and *Venus and Amor* (Basel, Offentliche
Kunstsammlung). When these paintings were in the
Amerbach collection they were said to represent the
artist's mistress, Magdalena Offenburg; her depiction
as Laïs of Corinth, the mistress of Apelles, was therefore
clearly appropriate. Both panels were at one time
attributed, significantly, to the Lombard artist Cesare
da Sesto, who died in Milan in 1523, and their
connection with Italian sources is plain. The gesture of
both *Laïs* and *Venus*, with their right hands outstretched, is close to that of Christ in Leonardo's mural
of *The Last Supper* in the Church of Santa Maria delle
Grazie, Milan; in addition, the use of *sfumato* modelling,
which can be seen as early as the *Amerbach* portrait
(Plate I), is yet more pronounced in these panels.
Numerous Italian characteristics in *The Meyer Madonna*,
painted in the same year and apparently also employing Magdalena Offenburg as the model for the
Madonna, have already been noted; in addition, the
extraordinarily soft modelling of the Christ Child and
the head of the Virgin in this altarpiece, and in the pair
of female half-lengths, might be used as evidence that
Holbein revisited Italy shortly before his first departure
for England in 1526. This use of *sfumato* modelling is

of 1516 (Plates 3 and 4) are the earliest dated works in
this genre. Meyer was elected Burgomaster of Basel in
the year in which his portrait was painted and was the
first commoner to hold this office; he must have been
well-known to Holbein for in the previous year the
artist had painted the Baer table-top (Plate 1) to
commemorate the wedding of the brother of Meyer's
first wife, Magdalena Baer, and about ten years later
Meyer commissioned an altarpiece from the artist for
the chapel of his castle near Basel (Plate VIII). The

fig. 7
Albrecht DÜRER (1471–1528)
Oswald Krel
Munich, Alte Pinakothek. 1499. Oil on panel
49·6 × 39 cm.

This portrait, one of Dürer's finest, is an
example of the kind of picture which must
surely have determined the formation of Holbein's portrait style. The particular type to
which it belongs follows that developed in the
Netherlands and much used in Italy around
the end of the fifteenth and beginning of the
sixteenth centuries, with an area of landscape
shown to the right or left and the sitter
depicted at half-length with his hand resting
on a ledge running parallel to the picture
plane in the foreground. Holbein apparently
never included a full landscape background in
his portraits, although there is the suggestion
of an alpine landscape in the potrait of *Bonifacius Amerbach* (Plate I). Otherwise the pose of
Holbein's sitters is very similar to that of
Dürer's *Oswald Krel*, for instance his depictions
of *Jakob Meyer* and *Dorothea Kannengiesser* (Plates
3 and 4), *Sir Thomas More* (Plate V) and *Derich
Born* (Plate VI). Holbein may in addition have
derived his skill in the depiction of textures,
and in particular fur, from the older artist.

contemporaneously is proved by the very beautiful
sheet of studies in the Louvre (Plate 25) which contains
a drawing of Erasmus's right hand as depicted in the
Louvre painting and of the left as shown in the picture
dated by Holbein (Plate 24). A third portrait of the
scholar, painted at around the same time, was taken by
Holbein to Amerbach in Montpellier in 1524. This
portrait is probably identifiable with the painting now

seen again from time to time in Holbein's portraits and
perhaps most notably in that of *Derich Born* of 1533
(Plate VI). But the dangers of employing the normal
stylistic criteria to place undated works in Holbein's
oeuvre are once again clearly appreciated when we note
that the portrait of *Georg Gisze*, dated 1532 (Plate 51),
makes little if any use of such modelling. The problem
is certainly aggravated by the uneven condition of
many of Holbein's paintings, in some of which the
surfaces are obscured by layers of varnish, while in
others layers of Holbein's own varnish have been
inadvertently removed. It may be no accident, however, that in the royal portraits of the later 1530s (Plates
XII, XIII and 71) the facial features of the sitters are
depicted with the most limited use of modelling by
softening shadow. Having made this observation one is
tempted to go further and to suggest that Queen
Elizabeth I's well-known dislike of deep shading in any
portrait likeness may have been inherited from her
father.

Holbein's reputation as a portraitist appears to have
been made to a large extent by his series of portraits of
Desiderius Erasmus painted in 1523. The scholar had a
great interest in supervising the painting, or drawing, of
his own likeness, which survives from the hands of
various artists (see fig. 8). When Erasmus wrote
introducing Holbein to Aegidius in Antwerp, he
suggested that the painter might visit Quentin Metsys,
who had executed a diptych containing portaits of
Aegidius and Erasmus as a gift from the sitters to More
in 1517 and who also designed a medal bearing the
likeness of Erasmus's head in 1519. In June 1524
Erasmus wrote to his, and Dürer's, friend Willibald
Pirkheimer at Nuremberg: 'Only recently I have again
sent two portaits of me to England, painted by a not
unskilful artist. He has also taken a portrait of me to
France.' That Holbein was the artist responsible for
these pictures is proved by a passage in a book
published by Froben in March 1526. This mentions
Holbein, who 'last year painted, most successfully and
finely, two portraits of our Erasmus of Rotterdam,
which he afterwards sent into England'. Other documents prove that Warham was the recipient of one of
the two portraits sent to England. The painting in the
Louvre (Plate 26), datable to 1523 on the basis of the
writing on which Erasmus is engaged, is usually
considered to be one of these, while the other, dated
1523, is identified as the panel which is now in a private
collection (Plate 24). These portraits show the scholar
writing and then in contemplation, in a format that is
ultimately derived from paintings and engravings
showing St. Jerome in his study. The scholar's profile in
the Louvre picture, outlined against the richly patterned curtain hanging behind him, has a sensational
power which is seldom equalled in Holbein's art. The
fact that the artist painted these two portraits virtually

fig. 8
Albrecht DÜRER (1471–1528)
Desiderius Erasmus
London, British Museum, Department of
Prints and Drawings. 1526. Engraving
24·9 × 19·3 cm.

Dürer's engraved portrait of *Erasmus* provides
yet another example of a likeness of the scholar, who appears to have taken a particular
interest in his own portraiture. This plate was
made three years after the main group of
portraits of Erasmus by Holbein (Plates 24
and 26), but probably on the basis of a sitting
in Antwerp in 1520. In a letter of 1528 Erasmus wrote: 'Pinxit me Durerius, sed nihil
simile' (Dürer painted my portrait, but it was
nothing like), and indeed were it not for the
similarities of pose and accompanying detail it
would be hard to believe that the man depicted here was the same as that shown by
Holbein.

in Basel, which repeats the sitter's pose from the Louvre
picture. When Holbein returned to the continent in
1530 he again painted Erasmus, by that time resident
in Freiburg. There are several undistinguished variants
of the privately owned panel which appear to date from
around this time and also the tiny roundel in Basel
which was painted as a companion to that of *Froben*,
now in the Merton collection. The last of Holbein's
portraits of Erasmus was a woodcut published in 1535,
the year before the scholar's death (Plate 111). It shows
him full-length, standing behind his personal emblem,
'Terminus', with a Latin inscription below, which
reads. in translation:

Pallas, marvelling at this picture to rival Apelles, says that a library
must preserve it for ever. Holbein shows his Daedalian art to the
Muses, and the great Erasmus [shows] the power of his supreme
intellect.

Such words of praise for the portrait painter's art were
surely not empty ones in the case of Holbein's likenesses
of Erasmus.

Apart from the panels discussed above, there are
comparatively few dated portraits from Holbein's hand
prior to his first visit to England, where he must have
been chiefly employed as a portraitist. The style of the
Italian Renaissance had already arrived in England by
1526, largely owing to the activities of Italian sculptors
and makers of ornaments, and in particular to Pietro
Torrigiano, who received the commissions to design the
tombs of Lady Margaret Beaufort and of King Henry
VII and his consort Elizabeth of York in 1511 and 1512
respectively. During his stay in England, which lasted
spasmodically until around 1522, Torrigiano executed
several portrait busts of sitters such as Henry VII and
his son Henry as a young man, John Fisher and Dean
Colet; a drawing by Holbein of the last survives among
his portraits at Windsor. Torrigiano recruited a
number of helpers during his absences from England in
Italy and, together with other documented artists such
as Benedetto da Rovezzano and Giovanni da Maiano,
they continued to operate in England until the mid-
1530s at least. So far as painting was concerned, the
Renaissance style had been brought over the Channel
by a handful of apparently rather second-rate artists
from both Italy and the Netherlands. Antonia Toto,
who was brought to England by Torrigiano, had served
his apprenticeship as a painter in the studio of Ridolfo
Ghirlandaio in Florence; according to Vasari he was
also the architect of Nonsuch, Henry VIII's great
palace in Surrey, begun in 1538 and destroyed late in
the seventeenth century. The names of Toto and
Bartolommeo Penni, 'paynters', occur in royal household accounts from 1530; in 1538 Toto became a
naturalized Englishman and five years later he succeeded as Sergeant-Painter, a position which he held
throughout Edward VI's reign. Although the careers of
these two artists are fairly well known on the basis of
documentary evidence, no painting can be attributed
to them with certainty, and there is no record of either
artist having painted portraits.

This is not the case, however, with the Flemings
Lucas and Gerard Horenbout, who are recorded as
having been in England shortly before Holbein's
arrival. In 1534 Lucas was nominated as the king's
painter, and ten years later he died in London.
According to van Mander, Holbein learnt the art of
miniature painting from 'Master Lukas' at the English
court, and although we know nothing certain of Lucas
Horenbout's *oeuvre* it seems highly probable that some
of the early miniatures of Henry VIII are from his hand,
and that he may have been a potential rival to Holbein

as a painter of portraits. It remains a fact, however, that there are no portraits of English sitters to equal those produced by Holbein during his residence in England.

Holbein's main work during his first visit to England was the magnificent group portrait of the family of Sir Thomas More, to whom the artist had been introduced by Erasmus. As is so often the case with key works by Holbein, the original painting, which was in distemper on canvas, was destroyed in the eighteenth century having been copied several times and also recorded by the artist in a drawing sent by him to Erasmus in Basel (Plate 29). In September 1529, on receipt of this study, the scholar wrote to More's eldest daughter, Margaret (Plate 92): 'so well has Holbein depicted the whole family for me that if I had been with you I could not have seen more'. Holbein's studies for nearly all of the people included in the group survive at Windsor Castle (Plates 30–35) and are fortunately among the best-preserved of the Holbein drawings there. Such a group portrait was unique at this time both north and south of the Alps, although the scenes painted by Mantegna depicting the Gonzaga family on the walls of the Camera degli Sposi in Mantua (fig. 4) may perhaps be relevant here. And if the concept of the entire composition was probably dependent on Italian proto-types, the poses of some of the individual figures, in particular that of More's daughter *Cecily Heron* (Plate 34), were close to other Italian models, for instance Leonardo's female portraits, including the *Mona Lisa* (Paris, Musée du Louvre) and *Cecilia Gallerani* (Kraków, Muzeum Narodowe). In addition to *The More Family Group*, Holbein painted a half-length portrait of More himself, dated 1527 (Plate V). In the same year he portrayed *Sir Henry Guildford* and *Lady Guildford* (Plates X and 37) and *William Warham, Archbishop of Canterbury* (Plate 36), and in the following year *Sir Thomas Godsalve and his Son John* (Plate 40) and the court astronomer *Nicolaus Kratzer* (Plate 41), who was responsible for the identifying inscriptions added to *The More Family Group* drawing sent to Erasmus. There is a richness and breadth in these portraits which continues throughout Holbein's English paintings.

Apart from the likenesses of *Erasmus* and *Froben* and the very similar one of *Melanchthon* (Plate 46), very few portraits can certainly be attributed to Holbein's stay in Basel between his two English visits. Thereafter the stream of dated works recommences with the striking group of studies of merchants of the German steelyard in London, by whom Holbein was chiefly employed in his early years after his return to England. The portraits of *Hans of Antwerp, Georg Gisze* and *A Member of the Wedigh Family* (Plates 50, 51 and 56) are all dated 1532, while those of *Hillebrandt Wedigh, Derich Tybis* and *Derich Born* (Plates 57, 52, 55 and VI) are dated 1533, as is that of *Robert Cheseman* (Plate 60) and the magnificent double portrait of the so-called '*Ambassadors*' (Plates IX,

53 and 54). In 1534 Holbein received an important commission to paint *Thomas Cromwell* (Plate 61), the King's Secretary, and following this he may have entered royal service. There follow the portraits of *King Henry VIII* and *Queen Jane Seymour* (Plates XII and XIII) of 1536–37, and those of the king's prospective brides *Christina of Denmark, Duchess of Milan* and *Anne of Cleves* (Plates VII and 72) in 1538 and 1539. We know from the written accounts of the negotiations in Brussels concerning the portrait of *Christina of Denmark* that it was painted on the basis of a sitting lasting only three hours on 12 March 1538. That evening Holbein set out on his return journey to England and on 18 March he showed the likeness of the young dowager duchess to the king in London. There was no time in between these dates for Holbein to have executed a finished oil painting of the size and quality of the picture in the National Gallery, London, and we must therefore presume that what he showed to the king was a portrait in pen and ink or coloured chalks, or even watercolour. The numerous portrait drawings at Windsor were presumably the results of sittings of similar length, an indication of Holbein's skill and facility as a portrait painter. The painting of *Christina* in London is Holbein's only surviving full-length, single-figure portrait and is a profoundly striking image. Her beauty was well-known and the kind was delighted with her likeness. However, the duchess, who had close Habsburg links, would not be lured by Henry and is reported to have said 'If I had two heads one would be at the disposal of the English majesty'. In the following year Holbein was therefore again at work recording the likenesses of possible brides for the king, this time in Düren, where he portrayed the Lutheran *Anne of Cleves* and her sister the Princess Amelia, whose portrait is lost. The painting of *Anne* in the Louvre (Plate 72) is on parchment laid down to a panel and may well represent the actual likeness that Holbein took of her at this time. This portrait is less successful than that of *Christina*, which may be partly due to the different technique and also to the fact that Anne of Cleves was by all accounts no great beauty.

Another important royal commission of around the same time as the *Christina of Denmark* portrait was the Privy Chamber painting for Whitehall Palace, executed c. 1536–37 and destroyed in the fire of 1698 but known from Leemput's copy (fig. 9); the cartoon for the figure of Henry VIII himself also survives (Plate 71). It is still not entirely clear where this painting was situated in the Privy Chamber, but it was definitely executed on the wall itself and would presumably have attempted to conform to the architecture of the room. The mural depicted King Henry VII and his wife Queen Elizabeth of York, with King Henry VIII and Queen Jane Seymour; the Latin inscription told of the father's victory over his foes to bring peace to the land

fig. 9
Remigius van LEEMPUT (d.1675)
Copy of Holbein's Whitehall Mural
Hampton Court Palace, Royal Collection.
1667. Oil on canvas 88·9 × 98·7 cm.

The central plinth records the original inscription on Holbein's painting and adds five lines to the effect that this copy was made on the orders of King Charles II, with the date 1667. The painting which this canvas records was executed by Holbein on the walls of the Privy Chamber of Whitehall Palace c.1536–37. The Whitehall mural was destroyed by fire in 1698, and Leemput's copy is one of the best records of its original appearance. The painting was a propaganda work for the Tudor dynasty and showed Kings Henry VII and Henry VIII with their consorts Elizabeth of York and Jane Seymour. Roy Strong's idea that it was raised high above the royal chair and canopy of state is unsatisfactory as, from such a distance, the great detail, which is clearly evident in the surviving fragment of the cartoon (Plate 71), would not have been visible, and further the perspective would not have matched up with the low viewpoint.

and the son's success in restoring religion. The figures were placed within a fictive architectural structure with a use of *all'antica* detail in the friezes and pilasters which were by now common in Holbein's work.

At the time of his death in 1543 Holbein was still working on the large composition of *King Henry VIII Granting the Charter to the Barber-Surgeon's Company* (Plate 94) which was completed posthumously by members of his studio. In this painting the king is shown to the left of centre with his own doctors Chambers and Butts by his right side and other members of the company ranged in two rather too well-ordered rows to his left. The part played by Holbein in the execution of this picture is confirmed by the X-ray of another version of the same composition held by the Royal College of Surgeons in London, which now appears to have been painted over Holbein's original cartoon, but in its present state the Barber-Surgeon's painting does the artist little credit.

Holbein's portraits can, in general, be divided into a few well-defined categories which persist throughout his mature work. To the first belong those in which the artist concentrated on the facial features of those portrayed, with comparatively little attention paid to potentially distracting details such as elaborate dress, background and accompanying objects. In its present state, the almost pathetic group portrait of *Holbein's Wife and Two Children* probably of 1528 (Plate IV), painted on paper and then applied to a panel, appears to belong to this category, although there was originally an architectural background which was cut away. The composition of this portrait is, incidentally, very close to various Madonna and Child groups by Leonardo. The chief representatives of this first category of portraiture are a large number of portraits dating from Holbein's second English period, including those of members of the Wedigh family (Plates 56 and 57) and *Sir Richard Southwell* (Plate 70). In these there was a gradual development in terms of the simplification of background, which came to have less and less texture and depth, while at the same time the sitters appear to have assumed increasingly static poses. It is fair to suggest that the quality of these portraits depends to a very large extent on the length of the sitting which the men and women depicted were prepared to grant to Holbein, but in the portrait of *Southwell* and the 1533 portrait of *Derich Born* (Plate VI) the artist achieved two of his most penetrating likenesses. Another example of the many Latin inscriptions in praise of Holbein's skill in verisimilitude occurs on Born's portrait and reads in translation: 'Here is Derich himself; add voice and you might doubt if the painter or his father created him.' The paintings of *King Henry VIII* and *Queen Jane Seymour* (Plates XII and XIII) and perhaps also those of *Edward, Prince of Wales* and *Charles de Solier, Sieur de Morette* (Plates 73 and 65) form a separate category for their purpose was rather different. In these paintings the whole figure was treated with uniform care, isolated in the midst of a neutral background, so that the finished effect is similar to that produced by an icon.

In other portraits the artist's intention was quite different and, while the sitter was no less diligently shown, the objects which surround him were so brilliantly and carefully depicted that they may well occupy the observer's entire attention. This is especially the case with the portraits painted early in Holbein's second English period, such as *Georg Gisze* of 1532 (Plate I) and *'The Ambassadors'* of 1533 (Plate IX), in which Holbein seems to have taken every opportunity to display his skill in distinguishing the different textures and layers of recession. The glass flask placed in front of Gisze's sleeve, for instance, appears to serve no very clear purpose except to have provided an opportunity to the painter to display his virtuosity in the depiction of velvet behind two layers of glass, or through the bunch of flowers. Ruskin particularly admired this portrait and wrote about it at length:

Gisze sits alone in his accustomed room, his common work laid out before him; he is conscious of no presence, assumes no dignity, bears no sudden or superficial look of care or interest, lives only as he lived—but for ever. It is inexhaustible. Every detail of it wins, retains, rewards the attention with the continually increasing sense of wonderfulness. It is also wholly true. So far as it reaches, it contains the absolute facts of colour, form, and character, rendered with an unaccusable faithfulness.

The commission to depict the French ambassador Jean de Dinteville and his friend Georges de Selve, Bishop of Lavaur, the so-called 'Ambassadors' (Plate IX) was used by Holbein for what is surely among his greatest *tours de force* as a painter. At the beginning of the twentieth century it was demonstrated that almost every item shown in this picture serves some very clear purpose in the elaborate programme. There are numerous *memento mori* symbols, typical of sophisticated Renaissance portraiture, for instance the curiously foreshortened skull in the foreground and that on Dinteville's cap brooch. In addition the exact time of day at which the men sat to Holbein can be calculated from the various instruments standing between the men on the buffet, while other objects must have been included to represent their interests. In the history of the portrait genre *'The Ambassadors'* must surely occupy a key position, as one of the boldest and most outspoken examples of a full-length double portrait ever painted.

Between these two types of portrait, the one with the figure isolated against a plain background, the other with the figure surrounded by a wealth of accumulated detail, is another category which contains many of Holbein's most penetrating portraits. Among these are the various studies of the artist's humanist friends from *Amerbach* (Plate I) to the several studies of *Erasmus* (Plates 24 and 26), those of *Froben* (Plate 12) and *More* (Plate V), in which the sitter is generally shown in a contemplatory attitude, or in the case of the Louvre *Erasmus* (Plate 26) actually composing one of his literary works.

In any discussion of Holbein's portraits the group of about eighty drawings in the Royal Library at Windsor Castle must play an important part. The studies range in date from those for *The More Family Group* (Plates 30–35) of 1526–28 to those of English courtiers and gentlemen with their wives produced in the last years of Holbein's life. The drawings were apparently mostly intended merely as preliminary studies to be developed into finished paintings at a later date, otherwise they would surely not have survived together but would have been scattered among the descendants of the sitters represented. However, the study of *John Godsalve* (Plate 39), as that of *Edward, Prince of Wales*, in Basel (Plate 74), appears to have been intended as a finished work in its own right. The group of drawings in the Royal Collection include most of the surviving portrait

fig. 10
Hans HOLBEIN the elder (c.1465–1524)
Jörg Bomheckel
Berlin, Staatliche Museen, Kupferstichkabinett.
Watercolour over silverpoint heightened with
white on prepared paper 13·9 × 10·1 cm.
Inscribed: jörg bomheckel.

This drawing is one of the group of sixty-nine
portrait studies by the elder Holbein preserved
at Berlin. They are datable to between 1509
and 1516, when the artist was still active in
Augsburg, and some have been identified in
inscriptions added by the artist. The technique
employed throughout this group of drawings
was silverpoint, with some use of white and
red chalk and watercolour, on prepared paper;
the same technique was used by the artist's
two sons Ambrosius and Hans the younger
throughout their careers. The portrait drawings by Holbein the elder in Berlin in many
ways represent a similar corpus to those by his
son in the Royal Collection.

fig. 11
Ambrosius HOLBEIN (c.1494–c.1519)
Head of a Young Man
Basel, Offentliche Kunstsammlung,
Kupferstichkabinett. 1517. Silverpoint and red
chalk with some watercolour on white
prepared paper 20 × 15·3 cm. Signed with
monogram and dated 1517.

This drawing was presumably executed in
Basel in 1517, the year in which Ambrosius
Holbein, Hans the younger's elder brother,
entered the painters' guild there. The fact that
it is both signed and dated suggests that it
may have been intended as a finished work.
The portraits by Ambrosius Holbein are in
general less penetrating than those of his
brother, and this is one of the few surviving
portrait drawings from his hand. The technique is very similar to that employed by
Hans Holbein the younger.

studies made during Holbein's two English visits. The
drawings were formerly gathered together in a 'Greate
Book', which was recorded in the collections of Edward
VI, Henry, Prince of Wales, and Charles I, as well as
those of the Lumley family and of the Earls of Arundel,
before finally returning to the Royal Collection at the
end of the seventeenth century. There are, however,
various stray drawings which must certainly date from
Holbein's time in England and which are now scattered
through public and private collections: the drawing of
Sir Nicholas Carew in Basel (Plate 45), that of *Morette* in

Dresden (Plate 64) and of the unknown *Scholar* or *Cler*
at Chatsworth (Plate 83) are among these.

It is generally claimed that the drawings from
Holbein's two English visits can be distinguished by th
different media employed, and it is possible to chec
this to a certain extent by linking the drawings to date
paintings in some cases. By this simple device,
appears that in the first period, to which the drawing
of members of the More family and those of *Guildfor*
(Plate 38) and *Warham* (Plate 36), belong, Holbei
employed black, white and coloured chalks, while in hi

second period, which certainly includes drawings such as those of the *Unknown Man* of 1535 (Plate 79), *Sir Richard Southwell* of 1536 (Plate 69) and *Queen Jane Seymour* of 1536–37 (Windsor Castle, Royal Collection), he used chalks, indian ink, applied with both pen and brush, and coloured washes on paper coated with a pink chalky preparation. But Holbein had himself used such a coated paper for his earliest drawings, for example the preparatory metalpoint studies for the 1516 pair of Meyer portraits in Basel, and both his father and brother used similar materials in their portrait studies (figs. 10 and 11). Indeed in Berlin there is a group of portrait drawings by Hans Holbein the elder employing this technique, to which the portrait of *Jörg Bomheckel* (fig. 10) belongs. The drawings were made during the artist's last years in Augsburg (c. 1509–16) and represent many of the citizens known to him there. None of these drawings was apparently worked up into an oil painting and they were instead intended as simple records, some of which were later used in crowd scenes in his religious paintings; the sitters in these drawings were in many cases identified by the artist himself. We may therefore conclude that the pink preparation of the paper in the drawings by Hans Holbein the younger of *Godsalve* and *Fisher* (Plates 39 and 43), for instance, which has formerly been used to date them to the second English period in spite of their similarity to earlier drawings, may instead be evidence of Holbein's continued use of prepared paper throughout his career, rather than of his readoption of the technique in c.1532 after having abandoned it about eight years earlier. In several of the Windsor drawings there has been a considerable amount of retouching, presumably to compensate for the loss of definition by the rubbing of the chalk outlines; in others there is a decline in quality, the inevitable result of the enormous number of portraits which Holbein was asked to paint during the 1530s and early 1540s. It has also been suggested that Holbein employed the so-called 'glass' method, as described by Dürer, to capture these likenesses, according to which the painter would trace the outlines of the sitter onto a pane of glass placed between himself and the subject. This would certainly help to account for the flattened impression created by some of the drawings. Various factors such as the poor condition of the drawings and the absence of comparative material in the form of contemporary portraits by other artists which might help us to date them on the basis of costume mean that it is seldom if ever possible to date those drawings whose sitters were not identified in the sixteenth century; the apparent lack of consistent stylistic development in Holbein's mature work is in fact confirmed by the internal evidence contained in these drawings. When all this has been said, however, the drawings at Windsor contain many passages of supreme quality, in the studies of the

More family in particular. As we should expect from the appearance of Holbein's finished paintings, he was meticulous in recording details of the fabric and pattern and in depicting the texture of materials so that we can guess from a very few strokes of the drawing instrument of what stuff a particular garment was made. The same sensitivity to texture can be seen in the lovely costume drawings (Plates 17 and 18), which were probably executed shortly before Holbein left Basel in 1526, and in the studies of animals from about the same time (Plates 22 and 23).

Holbein's activity as a miniature painter is as enigmatic as many of the other aspects of his career. His work in this genre is not documented but is described as of almost equal importance to his painting in oil by authorities such as Karel van Mander and Nicholas Hilliard. Van Mander stated that Holbein was taught the technique of miniature painting at the English court by 'the painter Lukas', who is generally identified as the equally enigmatic Flemish artist Lucas Horenbout. Van Mander continued: 'With Lukas he kept up mutual acquaintance and intercourse, and learned from him the art of miniature painting, which, since then, he pursued to such an extent, that in a short time he as far excelled Lukas in drawing, arrangement, understanding, and execution, as the sun surpasses the mon in brightness.' Hilliard's statement concerning Holbein as a miniaturist is perhaps even more revealing: 'Holbean's manner of limning I have ever imitated and howld it for the best.' Until one of the many miniatures of Thomas More based on Holbein's portraits is demonstrated to be an autograph work, all the surviving miniatures which can be ascribed to Holbein with some claim to authenticity appear to date from well into his second English period, that is from the time at which he is documented as a salaried servant of the crown. There are apparently no miniature portraits of members of the royal family from his hand, although *Solomon and the Queen of Sheba* (Plate 85) employs a miniaturist's technique, but the pair showing the sons of the first Duke of Suffolk called 'the Brandon boys' (Plates 86 and 87), the so-called '*Catherine Howard*' (Plate 89) and the *Lady Audley* (Plate 88), a work connected with a drawing at Windsor, clearly depict people belonging to the court circle. In addition to these, there is the group of self-portrait miniatures dated 1543 (Plate 91), the exquisite portrait of *Mrs. Pemberton* (Plate 90), and a handful of others possibly including the pair of *Margaret Roper* and *William Roper* (Plates 92 and 93).

Throughout his life Holbein provided designs for craftsmen involved in the decorative arts and for publishers. His work in these fields is less well-known today, although there is an important group of his drawings for painted glass in Basel and for jewellery, metalwork and armour in the British Museum. It is interesting in this connection that More specifically described Holbein as 'artifex' rather than 'pictor' in his letter to Erasmus of December 1526. While his designs for painted glass can chiefly be dated to the artist's residences in Lucerne and Basel in the late 1510s and early 1520s, his designs for metalwork all apparently belong to his second English period. The studies for painted glass, which were mostly executed in monochrome, include several religious scenes and in particular a series of ten Passion scenes (Plates 14 and 15), each carefully framed within a slightly different architectural border. There is also a large group of designs for heraldic windows in which the shield for a prospective patron's coat of arms is left empty (Plate 16). In the mature designs for glass, as in the woodcuts, there is a simplification of detail and a broadening of treatment to enable the drawings to be reproduced easily and, furthermore, to be understood at a distance by the observer.

Holbein's designs for metalwork, seals, garters, bookbindings and different types of jewellery are in many ways typical products of a sixteenth-century German artist. A large number of such designs survive by artists such as Peter Flötner (fig. 12), incorporating the same *all'antica* decorative vocabulary as that used by Holbein. Among the latter's best-known metalwork designs is that for a cup with Hans of Antwerp's name inscribed along the edge of the lid (Plate 96) suggesting that it was to be made for, or more probably by, Hans of Antwerp during the residence of both artists in London. The two designs for a decorated gold cup incorporating Jane Seymour's motto and the initials 'H' and 'I' bound by a loveknot are, not surprisingly, more elaborate (Plate 95) than the one for Hans's cup. From the evidence contained in the decoration on this cup it is fair to assume that it was in some way connected with Henry VIII's marriage to Jane in 1536; a cup that is certainly identifiable as the one made from these designs was recorded in royal inventories until it was pawned by Charles I in 1625 and then melted down four years later. The *Design for Sir Anthony Denny's Clock* (Plate 97) must have been among the artist's last works, for Denny inscribed upon it that the clock itself was given by him to the king as a New Year's gift in 1544, following Holbein's death. These studies reveal Holbein's skilful and meticulous yet fluid penwork in a way that his portrait studies only rarely do; these characteristics were noted at the outset of his career, in the marginal illustrations to Erasmus's *Encomium Moriae* (Plate 9), and by the artist's last years they were naturally further refined.

No finished product of Holbein's collaboration with goldsmiths, armourers and jewellers has apparently survived. The same is inevitably true of his decorative designs on a larger scale, about which there is tantalizingly little documentation. The decorative

fig. 12
Peter FLÖTNER (1485–1546)
Design for a Chair
Berlin, Staatliche Museen,
Kupferstichkabinett. Pen and wash
18·6 × 15·6 cm. Signed: PF/Loe/.

This drawing by Flötner is an example of designs by German artists for the applied arts roughly contemporary to those produced by Holbein in England. Flötner, like Dürer, was active chiefly in Nuremberg and produced an immense number of designs for metalwork and furniture. This drawing probably dates from the early 1520s.

schemes executed in Basel and Lucerne have already been discussed. In 1527, during the artist's first visit to England, several payments were made to 'Master Hans' in connection with temporary buildings at Greenwich, set up to house the celebrations for the new alliance between England and France. In his capacity as comptroller to the king, Henry Guildford, who was portrayed by Holbein about this time (Plate X), was responsible for the arrangements for these festivities, and from the wealth of *all'antica* decoration recorded in literary descriptions of these events it appears quite possible that Holbein may have been the artist involved; this would place his entry into royal service almost ten years earlier than the generally accepted date. Early in his second stay in England he was apparently commissioned by the merchants of the German steelyard to design a triumphal arch through which Queen Anne Boleyn would pass on her coronation procession on 31 May 1533. The form of the arch is recorded in a drawing in Berlin (Plate 59); above it Apollo is shown seated amongst the Muses and within a bower on which perches an eagle. On the actual triumphal arch the eagle assumed the form of an imperial emblem, with two heads, and this overt reference to imperial power was, not surprisingly, noticed and unfavourably commented upon by the royal participants in the procession. Holbein was doubtless also responsible for decorative schemes of a more lasting nature in palaces and houses in England, although there is very little surviving evidence of such work. One such record exists in a design for a chimney-piece for one of the royal palaces, which incorporates an elaborate allegorical scheme (Plate 100).

Holbein's activity in providing designs for publishers probably began during his apprenticeship, and his skill in this branch of art may have been one of the reasons why he and his brother Ambrosius moved from Augsburg to Basel in 1515. The pre-eminent place occupied by Basel for the printing of scholarly works dated from 1477, when Johann Amerbach, the father of Bonifacius, Holbein's friend (Plate I), set up his press there. Froben (Plate 12) learnt his trade under Amerbach and from 1491 to 1513 worked in partnership with him. During the first two decades of the sixteenth century an enormous quantity of scholarly works passed through the presses of Amerbach and Froben, and the latter was aided considerably by the presence in the town of scholars such as Erasmus, who acted as Froben's chief literary adviser at this time. Among Holbein's first important designs was the *Scaevola and Porsena* title-page (Plate 101) which was frequently re-used by Froben after its first appearance in 1516. But his designs for woodcuts can only be truly appreciated after around 1522, when Holbein worked in partnership with the brilliant woodcutter Hans Lutzelberger. The latter was responsible for cutting Holbein's designs for Luther's New Testament, published in 1522 (Plate 102) and the Old Testament series, published in 1538 but designed over ten years earlier (Plates 105–108), as well as many others. The quality of both the designing and the cutting of these woodcuts is superb. Holbein gradually abandoned any attempt at

creating a rich textural effect to equal that of Dürer's woodcuts, for instance, and aimed instead at a simplicity of line which succeeds in making his woodcuts monuments of that art. Once again his activity in this field was chiefly concentrated in his years in Basel, but he also provided designs for English publishers and was responsible for the title-page of the first complete English translation of the Bible, the Coverdale Bible, published in 1535 (Plate 104).

When Holbein died in 1543 his loss must have been felt even more profoundly in England than in Basel, and his presence was of tremendous significance to the evolution of British art. He left a large number of portraits to be copied and used as models by the few native artists, many of whom must have worked in his studio at various times. In addition, his designs for projects in publishing and the decorative arts were of great importance in providing inspiration to artists, goldsmiths and other craftsmen, while the influence of his larger decorative schemes can be seen in buildings even after the time of Inigo Jones. After Holbein the next English artist of real note was Nicholas Hilliard who was born four years after Holbein's death. Nevertheless in Hilliard's *The Arte of Limning*, written c. 1600, he expressed in a charming way the extent of the debt which both he and England owed to Holbein:

King Henry the eight a Prince of exquisit jugment and Royall bounty, soe that of cuning stranger even the best resorted unto him, and removed from other courts to his. Amongst whom came the most excelent Painter and limner Master Haunce Holbean the greatest Master Truly in both thosse arts after the liffe that ever was, so Cuning in both together and the neatest; and therewithall a good inventor, soe compleat for all three, as I never heard of any better than hee. Yet had the King in wages for limning Divers others, but Holbean's maner of limning I have ever imitated and howld it for the best, by Reason that of truth all the rare Siences especially the arts of Carving, Painting, Goudsmiths, Imbroderers, together with the most of all the liberall Siences came first unto us from the strangers, and generally they are the best and most in number. I heard Kinsard [?Ronsard] the great French poet on a time say, that the Ilands indeed seldome bring forth any Cunning man, but when they Doe it is in high perfection; so when I hope there maie come out of this ower land such a one, this being the greatest and most famous Iland of Europe.

BIBLIOGRAPHY

A. Chamberlain, *Hans Holbein the Younger* (London 1913).

H. von Einem, 'Holbeins "Christus im Grabe" ', *Abhandlungen der geistesund sozial-wissenschaftlichen Klasse 1960 der Akademie der Wissenschraften und der Literatur* (Mainz 1960).

Exhibition of Works by Holbein and other Masters (Royal Academy, London, exhibition catalogue 1950–51).

P. Ganz, *Die Handzeichnungen Hans Holbeins des Jüngeren* (Berlin 1937).

P. Ganz, *The Paintings of Hans Holbein* (London 1950).

H. W. Grohn, *Hans Holbein der Jüngere als Maler* (Leipzig 1955).

H. W. Grohn and R. Salvini, *L'opera pittorica completa di Holbein il Giovane* (Milan 1971).

F. Grossmann, 'Holbein Studies-I' and 'Holbein Studies-II', *The Burlington Magazine* (1951).

M. F. S. Hervey, *Holbein's 'Ambassadors'* (London 1900).

Holbein and the Court of Henry VIII (The Queen's Gallery, London, exhibition catalogue 1978–79).

'The King's Good Servant' Sir Thomas More (National Portrait Gallery, London, exhibition catalogue 1977–78).

M. Levey, *Holbein's 'Christina of Denmark, Duchess of Milan'* (London 1968).

Die Malerfamilie Holbein in Basel (Kunstmuseum, Basel, exhibition catalogue 1960).

M. Netter, 'Hans Holbein d. J. "Madonna des Bürgermeisters Jacob Meyer zum Hasen" und ihre Geheimnisse', *Basler Jahrbuch* (1951).

K. T. Parker, *The Drawings of Hans Holbein in the Collection of H.M. the King at Windsor Castle* (London 1945).

D. Piper, 'Holbein the Younger in England', *Journal of the Royal Society of Arts* (1953).

A. E. Popham, 'Hans Holbein's Italian Contemporaries in England', *The Burlington Magazine* (1944).

F. Saxl, 'Holbein and the Reformation', *A Heritage of Images* (London 1970).

H. A. Schmid, *Hans Holbein der Jüngere. Sein Aufstieg zur Meisterschaft und sein englischer Stil* (Basel 1948).

R. Strong, *Holbein and Henry VIII* (London 1967).

A. Woltmann, *Holbein und seine Zeit. Des Kunstlers Familie, Leben und Schaffen* (Leipzig 1874–76).

R. N. Wornum, *Some Account of the Life and Works of Hans Holbein* (London 1867).

1 Table-top for Hans Baer

ZÜRICH, Schweizerisches Landesmuseum. 1515. Tempera
on wood 102×136 cm. Signed and dated: HANS.HO
. . . 1515.

This table-top was painted to commemorate Hans Baer's
marriage on 24 June 1515. Baer was a citizen of Basel
and the brother-in-law of Jakob Meyer, whose portrait
Holbein painted in the following year (Plate 3). It
provides the earliest evidence of Holbein's presence in
Basel and is a fine example of the characteristically
German style which was spread chiefly through woodcuts
during the early years of the sixteenth century. The table-
top has also been attributed to Hans Herbst, another
painter active in Basel, with whom Holbein was associated at this time.

(*right*)
2 *The Flagellation of Christ*
BASEL, Offentliche Kunstsammlung. Tempera and oil on
canvas 137×115 cm.

The fact that *The Flagellation* is painted on canvas suggests that this painting and the four other similar Passion
scenes, also in Basel, were intended as temporary church
decoration, perhaps for Holy Week. There is an intensity
about this scene which probably indicates the influence of
Grünewald, and there are also features apparently derived
from Dürer's series of small woodcuts of scenes from the
Passion. The style seen in this early work seems to have
disappeared from Holbein's *oeuvre* around the mid-1520s
when his mature, polished style, rich in Italian influence,
replaced it.

23

3 *Jakob Meyer*
BASEL, Offentliche Kunstsammlung. 1516. Oil and tempera on wood 38·5×31 cm. Signed with a monogram and dated: 1516.

Jakob Meyer was elected Burgomaster of Basel in the year that this portrait was painted; he was the first commoner to hold this office. He was also the brother-in-law of Hans Baer for whom Holbein may have painted the table-top now in Zürich (Plate 1). Meyer married Dorothea Kannengiesser (Plate 4) as his second wife in 1513; their three children are shown with them and with Meyer's first wife in *The Meyer Madonna*, executed around ten years after this portrait (Plate VIII).

4 *Dorothea Kannengiesser*

BASEL, Offentliche Kunstsammlung. 1516. Oil and tempera on wood 38·5 × 31 cm.

This portrait was painted as the companion piece to that of *Jakob Meyer* (Plate 3), the sitter's husband, in 1516. The panels were formerly joined as a diptych, with the Meyer coat of arms on the outer face. Apart from the original physical linking of the two panels, they are also united by the architectural background and by the way in which the sitters look at one another.

(above left)
5 *Preliminary Study for the Overall Design of the Main Façade of the Haus zum Tanz*
BASEL, Offentliche Kunstsammlung, Kupferstichkabinett. Pen and ink with wash 53·7×36·5 cm.

The Haus zum Tanz in Basel, belonging to the goldsmith Balthasar Angelrot, was decorated with mural paintings by Holbein which were intended to cover the whole of the two street-fronts of the house. The main façade, for which this drawing was intended, was the shorter of the two and was situated on one of the major streets of Basel, the Eisengasse; the entrance to the house is shown on the left in the drawing. The extravagant foreshortening of the painted architecture was an attempt to compensate for the very limited space between this house and those on the opposite side of the street, a restriction which meant that the painted façades could be seen only with difficulty. This preliminary design has a freedom and fluency of handling typical of Holbein's mature style of draughtsmanship and seen to full advantage in his later designs for decorative objects (Plates 98 and 99). The Berlin drawing (Plate 6) is a more highly worked up version of this design, in which several details were altered. The Haus zum Tanz, with Holbein's other house-front decorations in Basel, was probably executed early in the 1520s; a copy of this drawing in Basel is dated 1520.

(above right)
6 *Overall Design for the Main Façade of the Haus zum Tanz*
BERLIN, Staatliche Museen, Kupferstichkabinett. Pen and ink with coloured washes 57·1×33·9 cm.

This drawing is a more highly finished and coloured version of the Basel study (Plate 5). It contains a characteristically German mixture of the sophisticated Italian Renaissance style, full of such detail *all'antica* as the triumphal arch in the background, with native German types seen in the musical peasant frieze above the ground-floor level.

(above left)
7 *Leaena and the Judges*
BASEL, Offentliche Kunstsammlung, Kupferstichkabinett. 1517–18. Pen and brown ink and wash
21·2 × 16·5 cm.

One of Holbein's chief commissions during his visits to Lucerne in 1517 and 1519 must have been
the internal and external decoration of the house belonging to the chief magistrate of the town,
Jakob von Hertenstein. Building work on the house was only completed in 1517; it remained
standing until 1825 and prior to its demolition in that year all surviving traces of Holbein's
paintings on the façade were copied by a group of local artists. From these copies it is possible to
reconstruct the original appearance of the house, which made free use of a number of Italian
decorative devices. The façade decorated by Holbein consisted of three principal storeys above a
ground floor; the first- and second-floor windows were decorative clusters of arms and armour and
above these windows was a triumphal procession, clearly derived from Mantegna's *Triumph of Caesar*
(fig. 3). Between the windows of the top storey were five scenes from ancient history evidently
chosen for their moral lesson: the space to left of centre was occupied by a depiction of the story of
Leaena and the judges, for which this drawing was the preparatory design. Leaena, the mistress of
the tyrant-slayer Aristogeiton, bit out her tongue to avoid the temptation of betraying her lover
during the trial.

(above right)
8 *Sapor and Valerian*
BASEL, Offentliche Kunstsammlung, Kupferstichkabinett. Pen and brown ink and wash with
watercolour 28·8 × 27·3 cm.

Holbein's decorations in the Great Council Chamber of Basel Town Hall were painted in two
stages, 1521–22 and c.1530, after his return from the first visit to England. The Rathaus, or Town
Hall, which was rebuilt in 1508–21, appears in the background of this drawing. Holbein's
decorative scheme consisted of scenes from ancient history and from the Old Testament, especially
chosen for the moral lessons they might provide to the councillors, set within a fictive architectural
framework; each scene was divided from the others by a niche containing an allegorical figure. On
either side of the finished painting of *Sapor and Valerian*, for which this drawing was a preliminary
sketch, were the figures of Wisdom and Temperance; the scene depicted is the humiliation of the
Emperor Valerian by Sapor, King of the Persians, who used him as a mounting block.

9 Marginal sketches in Erasmus's *Encomium Moriae*
BASEL, Öffentliche Kunstsammlung, Kupferstichkabinett. 1515–16. Pen and ink.

This detail, showing Folly descending the steps of a pulpit, is the last of several marginal sketches which Holbein and other artists added to a copy of Erasmus's *Encomium Moriae*, published by Froben in Basel in 1515 and belonging to the scholar Oswald Myconius, who left Basel for Zürich in 1516. It provides one of the first datable examples of Holbein's style of draughtsmanship and reveals that the fluency which is so much a mark of his later designs, in particular of those for the decorative arts, was already present in embryo at the outset of his career.

10 *Design for the von Hertenstein House*
BASEL, Öffentliche Kunstsammlung, Kupferstichkabinett. 1517–18. Pen and brown ink and wash with watercolour 30·7 × 44·7 cm.

Like *Leaena and the Judges* (Plate 7), this design was for the von Herstenstein house, decorated by Holbein during his residences in Lucerne in 1517 and 1519. The overall decorative scheme for the façade was clearly related to that of the Certosa at Pavia, south of Milan, completed in 1473, which Holbein could have visited during a trip to Italy around this time. The design incorporates the main entrance into the house and a window to one side and is full of illusionistic devices.

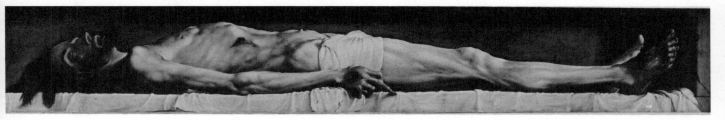

11 *Christ in the Tomb*

BASEL, Offentliche Kunstsammlung. 1521. Oil and tempera on panel 30·5 × 200 cm. Signed with monogram and dated: MDXXI.

This curious panel is described in the Amerbach inventory as 'A picture of a dead man with the title Jesus of Nazareth'. It may have formed the predella panel of an altarpiece of the same nature as Grünewald's *Isenheim Altarpiece* (Colmar, Musée d'Unterlinden) of c.1515, the predella panel of which also depicts the dead Christ. An alternative theory is that the painting may have taken the place of a piece of sculpture in an Easter Tabernacle. The flesh is depicted with an uncanny realism: the flesh-tints are green-grey in colour.

12 *Johannes Froben*

WINDSOR CASTLE, Royal Collection. c.1522–23. Oil on panel 55·2 × 32·4 cm., including a later addition at the top of 6·4 cm.

The printer Johannes Froben (1460–1527) was painted by Holbein in Basel c.1522–23 and this painting therefore belongs to the same period as the portraits of *Erasmus* (Plates 24 and 26). With the elder Amerbach, Froben was the most important printer in Basel at this time, and many of his books of the second and third decades of the sixteenth century were illustrated with designs by Holbein (Plates 101 and 103) and his brother Ambrosius. During his years of residence in Basel Erasmus acted as literary adviser to Froben, and it is probable that it was Froben who first introduced Holbein to the scholar. This portrait may have been incorporated with one of Erasmus in a diptych recorded c.1600. The companion piece would have been the portrait of *Erasmus* in the Royal Collection: the original background behind Froben, now painted over but visible in X-ray photographs, includes a curtain which also appears in that portrait of *Erasmus*. In the late 1620s the background of the *Froben* portrait was painted in by Hendrick van Steenwyck the younger, who was patronized both by the Duke of Buckingham and King Charles I, to whom the pictures were presented by Buckingham in 1627.

13 *The Solothurn Madonna*

SOLOTHURN, Museum der Stadt Solothurn. 1522. Oil and tempera on panel 140·5 × 102 cm. Signed with monogram and dated: 1522.

The Virgin is shown seated beneath a simple tunnel-vaulted structure with St. Nicholas and St. Ursus at either side. The figures are of a rather bulky and static form and, as in *The Meyer Madonna* of about five years later (Plate VIII), they do not occupy more than the foreground plane. In this respect the composition departs from its north Italian models. The altarpiece was painted for Hans Gerster, the town archivist of Basel, and appears to use the features of Holbein's wife (Plate IV) for those of the Virgin.

(right)
16 *Design for a Painted Glass Window with Two Unicorns*
BASEL, Offentliche Kunstsammlung, Kupferstichkabinett.
Pen and ink with wash and watercolour 42×31·7 cm.

This drawing is one of a group of studies for heraldic
windows designed by Holbein during his residence in
Basel. These designs display a simplicity of outline and
contour common to all Holbein's mature work in this
genre, and the architecture has a sophistication typical of
the best northern art of c.1525, comparable to that seen,
for instance, in Mabuse's *Hercules and Dejanira* of 1516
(Birmingham, Barber Institute of Fine Arts).

(above left)
14 *Design for a Painted Glass Window with the Mocking of
Christ*
BASEL, Offentliche Kunstsammlung, Kupferstichkabinett.
Pen and ink with wash 43·2×30·9 cm.

This drawing is one of a set of ten designs for painted
glass windows with Passion scenes. It has an intensity of
feeling typical of one aspect of Holbein's early style,
which was clearly influenced by Grünewald.

(above right)
15 *Design for a Painted Glass Window with Pilate Washing his
Hands*
BASEL, Offentliche Kunstsammlung, Kupferstichkabinett.
Pen and ink and wash 43·3×31 cm.

This drawing is another of the group of designs for
painted glass Passion scenes. These designs were for
painted rather than stained glass. The artist would paint
on white glass which would then be re-fired. The panes of
glass thus produced were used in both sacred and secular
settings.

(*above left*)
17 *Costume Study: Noblewoman*
BASEL, Offentliche Kunstsammlung, Kupferstichkabinett. Ink applied with pen and brush and wash 29·1 × 19·8 cm.

(*above right*)
18 *Costume Study: Lady of the Bourgeoisie*
BASEL, Offentliche Kunstsammlung, Kupferstichkabinett. Ink applied with pen and brush and wash 29·1 × 19·9 cm.

Both drawings come from a group of five sheets of costume studies, two of noble dress, two of bourgeois dress and one of courtesans' dress. They are valuable documents for the history of fashion and are comparable to those made by Dürer during his Netherlandish journey about five years before these drawings were executed by Holbein c.1526. The noblewoman (Plate 17) wears a bridal cap, presumably for her own wedding, and a jewel hung from a collar inscribed, appropriately, with the words 'AMOR VI[NCIT]'.

(*opposite*)
I *Bonifacius Amerbach*
BASEL, Offentliche Kunstsammlung. 1519. Oil on panel 28·5 × 27·5 cm. Signed and dated:
IO.HOLBEIN.DEPINGE BAT.A.M.D.XIX.PRID.EID.OCTOBR.

This portrait was painted in the year that Amerbach, the son of a famous Basel printer and publisher, returned to his home town from Freiburg, where he had been studying. He was a considerable scholar and was awarded the chair in Roman Law at Basel University in 1525. Amerbach may first have met Holbein through Erasmus and his friendship with the artist continued throughout their lives; the vast collection of works by Holbein that Amerbach formed was the basis for the corpus of Holbein material in the Offentliche Kunstsammlung. This is the most striking portrait from Holbein's early years and it developed a formula frequently seen in Italy and in the art of Albrecht Dürer. The inscription attached to the tree is chiefly in praise of Holbein's skill in verisimilitude and is of a type frequently found in Holbein's pictures. To achieve this life-like effect the artist employed the *sfumato* technique which he must have learnt during his presumed but undocumented visit, or visits, to Italy.

19 *The Passion Altarpiece*
BASEL, Offentliche Kunstsammlung. c.1524. Oil and tempera on panel. Total height: 149·5 cm.; width of individual panels: 31 cm.

This so-called altarpiece may in fact represent the shutters of an actual altarpiece which has not survived. The eight individual scenes of the Passion are represented with striking intensity of colour within the arched shape of the frame. It is undated but probably comes from early in the 1520s.

(opposite)
II *Noli Me Tangere*
HAMPTON COURT PALACE, Royal Collection. Oil on panel 76·7 × 95·2 cm.

This panel is curiously difficult to date, and its presence in England indicated to some of Holbein's biographers that it belonged to one of the artist's periods of residence there. Owing to the iconoclasm in Basel there are no strictly comparable works from his years in Switzerland, but the similarity of the brilliant lighting effects and the Grünewald-like intensity suggest that *Noli Me Tangere* is close in date to *The Passion Altarpiece* of c.1524 (Plates 19–21).

(above left)
20 *The Passion Altarpiece: Christ on the Mount of Olives*, detail of Plate 19.

This scene occupies the top left-hand area of *The Passion Altarpiece*. The image is presented with great simplicity, and the main effect is made by the celestial light falling from the right on Christ's face and shoulder and on the sleeping forms of the Apostles in the foreground.

(above right)
21 *The Passion Altarpiece: The Crucifixion*, detail of Plate 19.

The Crucifixion appears as the penultimate of the eight Passion scenes, to right of centre in the lower row of *The Passion Altarpiece*. There are numerous features which appear to have been influenced by Italian art, from the form and technique of the crucified figure to the poses of soldiers standing in the foreground.

22 *Study of Lambs*
BASEL, Offentliche Kunstsammlung, Kupferstichkabinett. Watercolour and wash 20·7 × 24·6 cm

23 *Study of a Bat*
BASEL, Offentliche Kunstsammlung, Kupferstichkabinett. Watercolour and wash 16·6 × 27·9 cm.

These studies are generally ascribed to Holbein's residence in Basel and are similar in many ways to the elder Holbein's studies of animals now preserved in the museums of Erlangen, Bamberg and Basel, among others.

 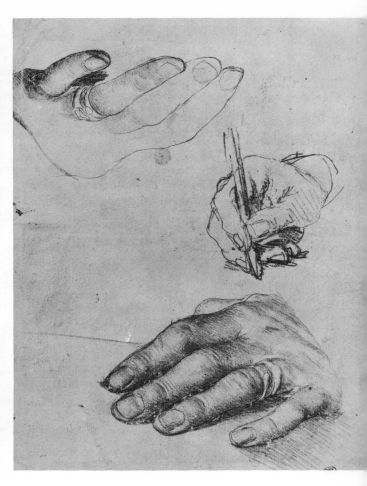

(*above left*)
24 *Desiderius Erasmus*
Private collection. 1523. Oil on panel 76·2 × 51·4 cm.

This painting is dated 1523 on the cover of one of the books on the shelf in the top right-hand corner and is probably to be identified with one of the two portraits which Erasmus sent to England before June 1524, one of which was a gift for Warham (Plate 36). The Greek inscription along the book held by Erasmus reads in translation: 'the Herculean Labours of Erasmus of Rotterdam'. The Latin couplet on the edge of the book that bears the inscribed date refers to Holbein's powers of portraiture in complimentary terms and was presumably composed by Erasmus himself: '[IL]LE EGO IOANNES HOLBEIN NON FACILE [VLL]VS [TAM] MICH[MIMVS] ERIT QVAM MICHI[MOMVS] ERAT.'

(*above right*)
25 *Studies of Hands*
PARIS, Musée du Louvre, Cabinet des Dessins. 1523. Silverpoint and black and red chalk on prepared paper 20·6 × 15·5 cm.

This sheet of studies provides one of the pieces of evidence that the two portraits of *Erasmus* by Holbein (Plates 24 and 26) were executed very close in time. The study of the right hand was used for the Louvre painting, and those of the left were used for the other painting.

(*opposite*)
26 *Desiderius Erasmus*
PARIS, Musée du Louvre. 1523. Oil on panel 43 × 33 cm.

One of several portraits painted by Holbein of Erasmus, this panel was almost certainly executed in 1523 when both the artist and the sitter were resident in Basel. They became close friends, and it was through Erasmus that Holbein met Sir Thomas More during the artist's first visit to London. In contrast to the previous portrait (Plate 24), the scholar is here shown in pure profile as he is represented, for instance, on the medal of c.1519 designed by Quentin Metsys. The writing on the sheet of paper in front of Erasmus is clearly legible as the opening words of his *Commentary on the Gospel of St. Mark*, on which he was working in 1523. This painting has been identified as the second portrait despatched by Erasmus to England in 1524.

(*above left*)
27 *Kneeling Figure of Jeanne de Boulogne, duchesse de Berry*
BASEL, Offentliche Kunstsammlung, Kupferstichkabinett. c.1524. Black and coloured chalks
39·6 × 27·5 cm.

(*above right*)
28 *Kneeling Figure of Jean de France, duc de Berry*
BASEL, Offentliche Kunstsammlung, Kupferstichkabinett. c.1524. Black and coloured chalks
39·6 × 27·5 cm.

Holbein's journey to France in 1524 is recorded in a letter by Erasmus stating that the artist had taken a portrait of him to France; the visit is confirmed on the evidence provided by these two drawings depicting the kneeling figures which were at that time on either side of the High Altar of the Sainte Chapelle in the palace at Bourges; the figures were partially destroyed during the French Revolution. These drawings apparently represent Holbein's first use of black and coloured chalks on unprepared paper and are very beautiful and carefully worked examples of that technique. It is suggested that he learnt this method of draughtsmanship during his visit to France and his use of it is conspicuous in the five or so years after his visit: the preparatory studies for *The Meyer Madonna* (Plate VIII) are in coloured chalks, as are the drawings for *The More Family Group* (Plates 30–35) and other studies datable to Holbein's first English visit. At the time of his French visit Holbein had already been using chalk as a drawing instrument for some time, but always on coated paper, as in the studies of hands (Plate 25) for the *Erasmus* portraits of 1523.

29 *The More Family Group*

BASEL, Offentliche Kunstsammlung, Kupferstichkabinett. 1528. Pen and ink 38·8 × 52·4 cm.
Inscribed overall by both Holbein and Nicolaus Kratzer.

This drawing provides us with the best evidence for the final appearance of Holbein's lost painting
of the family of Sir Thomas More, seated in their house in Chelsea. The painting itself, executed in
tempera on linen or canvas, was the major work of Holbein's first English stay from 1526 to 1528;
it was destroyed by fire in the eighteenth century but is also recorded in several later versions in
oil. This drawing was taken from London to Erasmus in Basel, probably by the artist himself. The
annotations are mostly in the hand of Nicolaus Kratzer, tutor to More's household (Plate 41): he
noted the age and identity of each sitter. Another hand, perhaps that of Holbein himself, noted
that the hanging viol should be replaced by musical instruments lying on the buffet and that
Dame Alice should sit instead of kneel. Such suggestions, coupled with the possibility that Holbein
himself transported the drawing to Basel, provide some evidence that the painting was unfinished
when Holbein left England in 1528. In September 1529 Erasmus wrote both to More and to
More's eldest daughter Margaret Roper (Plate 92), expressing his admiration for Holbein's skill in
portraying his dear friends: 'so well has Holbein depicted the whole family for me that if I had
been with you I could not have seen more'. The drawings of members of the More family in the
Royal Collection (Plates 30–35) are preparatory studies for the destroyed painting.

Tho: Moor L^dChancelour

(above left)
31 *Sir John More*
WINDSOR CASTLE, Royal Library. 1526–28. Black and coloured chalks 35·1 × 27·3 cm.

Sir John was Thomas More's father and an important lawyer. Thomas was his second child and the eldest son of Sir John's first marriage and provided a home for his father during his later years.

(above right)
32 *John More the younger*
WINDSOR CASTLE, Royal Library. 1526–28. Coloured chalks 38·1 × 28·1 cm.

John More was the only son and youngest child of Sir Thomas More. He is portrayed here as he appeared in *The More Family Group*, in which he was shown with his future wife, Anne Cresacre (Plate 33), whom he married in 1529. The drawing displays a freedom of touch and handling, for instance in the sleeve and hand, seldom found in the protrait drawings at Windsor.

(opposite)
30 *Sir Thomas More*
WINDSOR CASTLE, Royal Library. 1526–28. Black and coloured chalks 39·7 × 29·8 cm.

This study is connected with both *The More Family Group* (Plate 29) and the independent half-length portrait of *More* in the Frick Collection (Plate V). Holbein had been introduced to More through their mutual friend Erasmus, who like Holbein had spent much of his time in England resident in More's house. By the time that the artist reached England in 1526 he had already worked on providing illustrations for some of More's writings (Plate 101). The outlines of this drawn portrait have been pricked, apparently for transfer to a panel or canvas.

33 *Anne Cresacre*
WINDSOR CASTLE, Royal Library. 1526–28. Black and coloured chalks 37·3 × 26·7 cm.

Anne Cresacre, an only child and the heiress of Edward Cresacre of Yorkshire, was one of Thomas More's many wards, and at the time of the painting of *The More Family Group* she was betrothed to his son, John, whom she married in 1529. The couple produced several children.

34 *Cecily Heron*
WINDSOR CASTLE, Royal Library. 1526–28. Coloured chalks 39 × 28·2 cm.

Cecily Heron was the third and youngest daughter of Sir Thomas More. She married Giles Heron in 1525. More's last letter, written to his eldest daughter Margaret Roper on the eve of his execution, contains the following passage: 'Recommend me when ye may to my good daughter Cecily, whom I beseech our Lord to comfort. And I send her my blessing, and to all her children, and pray her to pray for me. I send her a handkerchief and God comfort my good son her husband.' Cecily's pose and appearance in this drawing and in the Basel study of the group (Plate 29) suggest that she was pregnant at the time of the painting. It is possible that her pose was derived from that in Leonardo's portrait of *Cecilia Gallerani*.

(*above left*)

35 *Elizabeth Dauncey*

WINDSOR CASTLE, Royal Library. 1526–28. Black and coloured chalks. 36·8 × 26 cm.

Elizabeth was Sir Thomas's second daughter; she married in 1525, on the same day as her younger sister Cecily (Plate 34). This drawing is also a preparatory study for *The More Family Group* in which Elizabeth Dauncey was shown standing. The misleading inscription 'The Lady Barkley' is by a later hand.

(*above right*)

36 *William Warham, Archbishop of Canterbury*

WINDSOR CASTLE, Royal Library. 1527. Black and coloured chalks 40·1 × 31 cm.

William Warham (c.1450/56–1532) was a close friend of Erasmus and must consequently have met Holbein soon after the artist's arrival in England. In 1524 Erasmus had sent Warham a portrait of himself painted by Holbein, and the portrait of Warham, for which this drawing was a preparatory study, was intended as a gift for Erasmus. The portrait of *Warham* in the Louvre, dated 1527, is generally identified with this painting. It is probably significant that the pose adopted by Warham in this picture is very close to that of *Erasmus* (Plate 24), which may formerly have belonged to Warham. He was appointed Archbishop of Canterbury in 1502 and in this office clashed with Wolsey, who was Archbishop of York, but they worked together for Henry VIII's divorce from Queen Catherine of Aragon, although they both died before it was finalized.

37 *Mary Wotton, Lady Guildford*
ST. LOUIS, St. Louis Art Museum. 1527. Oil on panel 87 × 70·5 cm. Inscribed and dated: ANNO
MDXXVII AETATIS SVAE XXVII.

This portrait was painted as a pendant to that of *Sir Henry Guildford*, the sitter's husband (Plate X).
There is a drawing of Lady Guildford in Basel in which she is similarly dressed but assumes a more
frontal pose.

(*above left*)
38 *Sir Henry Guildford*
WINDSOR CASTLE, Royal Library. 1527. Black and coloured chalks with some watercolour
38·8 × 29·8 cm.

This drawing is a preparatory study for Holbein's painting of *Guildford* dated 1527 (Plate X). The study cannot have been transferred directly to the panel for there the face is enlarged in scale and slightly altered in countenance.

(*above right*)
39 *John Godsalve*
WINDSOR CASTLE, Royal Library. c.1528. Black and coloured chalks, black ink applied with pen and brush, watercolour and bodycolour on pink prepared paper 36·7 × 29·6 cm.

In the past this drawing was held to have been almost entirely overpainted, but this is not now thought to be the case. The drawing and modelling in the face are certainly of the highest quality, and the protrait has a degree of finish, particularly in the inclusion of details such as a foreground ledge, suggesting that it was not intended as a preparatory work for another picture but rather, like the portrait of *Edward, Prince of Wales, with a Monkey* (Plate 74), was a work of art in itself. No related painting is known, although the sitter appears in another portrait, attributed to Holbein, in the Johnson Collection in the Philadelphia Museum of Art and with his father Thomas in an autograph work of 1528 in Dresden (Plate 40). On the basis of its technique this drawing is generally dated to early in Holbein's second English period. It is quite possible, however, that Holbein continued to use a chalky preparation for his drawings, albeit intermittently, throughout the later 1520s and so this drawing may be dated c.1528. The sitter's age does not appear to be radically different to that in the Dresden double portrait.

· Anno · Dni · M · D · XXVII ·

40 *Sir Thomas Godsalve and his Son John*
DRESDEN, Staatliche Gemäldegalerie. 1528. Oil on panel 35 × 36 cm. Inscribed and dated: Thomas
Godsalve de Norwico Etatis sue Anno quadragesimo septo.

This painting, like the portrait of *Kratzer* (Plate 41), is dated 1528 and therefore was executed at
the end of Holbein's first stay in England. Thomas Godsalve was a Norfolk landowner and an
intimate friend of Thomas Cromwell, who was apparently responsible for furthering the career of
his son John: in November 1531 the elder Godsalve wrote to Cromwell thanking him for kindnesses
shown to his son and sending him 'half a dozen swans of my wife's feeding'. John Godsalve held
several minor offices under Henry VIII before being knighted in 1547 and appointed Comptroller
of the Mint in the reign of Edward VI. He had connections with the German steelyard, for which
Holbein worked during the early years of his second visit, and was portrayed by Holbein in
another pose in a drawing at Windsor (Plate 39).

(*opposite*)
III *Laïs Corinthiaca*
BASEL, Offentliche Kunstsammlung. 1526. Oil on panel 35·6 × 26·7 cm. Inscribed and dated:
LAIS:CORINTHIACA:1526.

Laïs Corinthiaca and its pendant *Venus and Amor*, also in the Offentliche Kunstsammlung, are
described in the 1586 catalogue of the Amerbach collection as 'Zwie täfelin doruf eine Offenburgin
conterfehet ist vf eim geschriben Lais Corinthiaca, die ander hat ein Kindin by sich.' The model
for both of these paintings is, therefore, identifiable as the artist's mistress, Magdalena Offenburg,
who is appropriately shown here in the guise of Laïs of Corinth, the mistress of Apelles. On the
basis of this identification it appears that Magdalena Offenburg also posed for the Virgin in *The
Meyer Madonna* (Plate VIII). The two paintings are rich in Italian references and in particular to
works by Leonardo, from whose art Holbein must surely have learnt the *sfumato* technique which is
such a striking feature of the *Laïs*.

(*opposite*)
IV *Holbein's Wife and Two Children*
BASEL, Offentliche Kunstsammlung. Oil on paper, backed on wood 77 × 64 cm. Inscribed: 152(?).

This life-size portrait group was originally painted on four sheets of paper, and at a later date the
figures were cut around and the whole was mounted on a panel. The original background
destroyed at this time was similar to that seen in early portraits such as those of *Jakob Meyer* and
Dorothea Kannengiesser (Plates 3 and 4), with pilasters and an ornamented frieze. The last figure of
the date in the inscription was also cut away at this time, but the painting is normally assigned to
the period after Holbein's return to Basel following his first visit to England, on the basis of the
ages of his children. While Holbein was working in London his family continued to reside in Basel,
where the artist visited them only very occasionally. His will, made shortly before his death in
1543, provided for two infants who were presumably his illegitimate offspring in London. The
composition of this picture surely derived from Italian prototypes and in particular from paintings
employing pyramidal groupings evolved by Leonardo and Raphael during the first decade of the
sixteenth century.

(*page 52*)
V *Sir Thomas More*
NEW YORK, Frick Collection. 1527. Oil on panel 74·2 × 59 cm. Inscribed: M.D.XXVII.

This portrait is almost certainly identifiable as the picture painted by Holbein in London in 1527;
X-rays taken in 1952 reveal that the position of the head changed during the painting. Here More
appears in his late forties, in a pose similar to that in which he was shown in the group portrait of
his family (see Plate 29), which was contemporary to this panel. Holbein's connection with More,
to whom he was introduced by Erasmus, was crucial to the success of his first visit to England.
More became a member of the king's council in 1517, hence the collar of 'SS' around his neck, and
four years later he was knighted and appointed Sub-Treasurer. His appointment as Lord
Chancellor in 1529, following the fall of Wolsey, was short-lived for, an intensely religious man, he
could not agree to Henry VIII's divorce. He therefore resigned his office in 1532, the year of
Holbein's return to England; two years later he was committed to the Tower and in July 1535 he
was executed.

41 *Nicolaus Kratzer*

PARIS, Musée du Louvre. 1528. Oil on panel 83 × 67 cm. Inscribed and dated: Imago ad vivam effigiem expressa Nicolai Kratzeri monasensis 9 [i] bavarus erat quadragessimu [primu] annu tpre [tempore] illo [com]plebat 1528.

Nicolaus Kratzer left his native Germany for England in 1517–18 and by 1520 had entered the king's service as an astronomer; he appears to have continued in royal employment until the time of his death around the middle of the sixteenth century. In 1521 More described Kratzer as 'a great friend of mine and very skilled in astronomy', and he gave lessons in mathematics and astronomy to members of More's household. Kratzer was probably responsible for adding the names and ages of the sitters to the drawing of *The More Family Group* presented by More to Erasmus (Plate 29). In 1520 he had been present at one of Erasmus's sittings to Dürer in Antwerp (fig. 8). Among King Henry's New Year's gifts in 1529 was a manuscript of Nicolaus Kratzer's *Canones Horoptri* which was written out by Peter Meghen and decorated by Holbein; it is now in the Bodleian Library, Oxford.

(above left)
42 *Unknown Lady with a Squirrel*
KINGS LYNN, Houghton Hall, collection of the Marquess of Cholmondeley. Oil on panel
54 × 38·7 cm.

The identity of the sitter in this charming portrait is not known but it is probable that the portrait
dates from Holbein's first English period. The fur hat which she wears is similar to one worn by
Thomas More's adopted daughter, Margaret Giggs, in *The More Family Group* (Plate 29).

(above right)
43 *John Fisher*
WINDSOR CASTLE, Royal Library. Black and coloured chalks, reinforced with brush and pen and
black ink, with some watercolour on pink prepared paper 38·3 × 23·4 cm. Inscribed and dated in a
contemporary hand: Il Epyscop° de roscster fo . . . ato Il Capo lano 1535.

A generation younger than Warham, Fisher was appointed Bishop of Rochester in 1504; owing to
his opposition to the royal divorce he was imprisoned in 1534 and executed in the following year,
as the inscription states. At the time of Holbein's return to England in 1532 Fisher was already out
of favour and it is therefore unlikely that this portrait was drawn then, in spite of the fact that the
pink priming and watermark of the paper are similar to those of other drawings dating from
Holbein's second English period. It is very probable that Holbein did not temporarily abandon the
use of coloured preparations for his drawings c.1524–32, as has been thought, and there is therefore
no reason why this drawing should not have been produced during the artist's first visit.

44 *Thomas Boleyn, first Earl of Wiltshire and of Ormond*
WINDSOR CASTLE, Royal Library. Black and coloured chalks, black ink applied with pen and brush
and watercolour on pink prepared paper 40·5 × 29·4 cm.

Owing to the inscription 'Ormond', this drawing is usually said to represent Anne Boleyn's father,
the Treasurer of the Household in 1522 and Lord Privy Seal in 1530. No surviving picture can be
connected with this drawing, which is among the most striking of Holbein's portrait studies, both
in terms of colour and of technique. The free handling of the drapery, in brush and indian ink, is
comparable to that in black chalk in the drawing of *John More the younger* (Plate 32), although the
Boleyn portrait shows markedly more meticulous treatment of the facial features and hair. On the
basis of technique this study has generally been dated c.1535, although a date somewhat earlier
and less close to his daughter's disgrace might make the identification more likely. If this drawing
was, in fact, executed during Holbein's first English period then Boleyn would have been in his late
forties, which seems a quite likely age for this sitter.

(above left)
45 *Sir Nicholas Carew*
BASEL, Offentliche Kunstsammlung, Kupferstichkabinett. Black and coloured chalks 55 × 38·6 cm.

This drawing is related to the painting at Drumlanrig Castle (Plate XI), but appears to have been executed some time before work began on that portrait. The style of the drawing suggests that it belongs to the first English period, while the oil painting, which does not in any case follow the pose of the drawings, must be later. It therefore seems that the drawing was made before Holbein left for Basel in 1528, but was never used for a finished work, and that the painting was executed on the artist's return to England four years later.

(above right)
46 *Philip Melanchthon*
HANOVER, Niedersächsische Landesgalerie. c.1530. Oil on panel 9 cm. (diameter). Inscribed on verso: QVI CERNIS TANTVM NON VIVA MELANTHONIS ORA HOLBINVS RARA DEXTERITATE DEDIT.

This tiny portrait of the German theologian and reformer is one of the few works by Holbein that can be dated between his two English visits, c.1530. It is of a very similar format to roundels of *Erasmus* (Basel, Offentliche Kunstsammlung) and *Froben* (Merton collection) also painted about this time and may have been intended to form part of a group with these works. Both in format and in the hard modelling of the facial features this portrait has much in common with works by Dürer, for instance the portrait of *Johannes Kleberger*, (Vienna, Kunsthistorisches Museum) dated 1526.

(opposite top)
47 *Rehoboam Rebuking the Elders*
BASEL, Offentliche Kunstsammlung, Kupferstichkabinett. 1530. Pen and ink with wash and watercolour 22·6 × 38·5 cm.

The composition on the wall of the Great Council Chamber of the Basel Town Hall, showing Rehoboam rebuking the elders, was not painted until 1530, in between Holbein's two English visits. Surviving fragments of the mural (Plate 48) reveal that when it was painted several changes were made to this preparatory composition. The story was taken from I Kings:12 which recounts how before his accession, Rehoboam, King of Shechem, consulted both his father's old councillors and the companions of his youth as to how he should treat the people. When on the throne he followed the advice of his young friends, who had recommended harshness, and rebuked the cold councillors who had advised mildness. The overall composition of this design is fairly similar to that of the *Solomon and the Queen of Sheba* miniature (Plate 86), to which it is also probably close in date.

(opposite bottom)
48 *Rehoboam Rebuking the Elders*, fragment
BASEL, Offentliche Kunstsammlung. 1530. Fresco secco 28 × 41·5 cm.

This is one of several fragments of the *Rehoboam* composition removed from the walls of the Great Council Chamber and now preserved in the Offentliche Kunstsammlung.

49 *Samuel and Saul*
BASEL, Offentliche Kunstsammlung, Kupferstichkabinett. c.1530. Pen and ink with wash and watercolour 21·5 × 53·5 cm.

As with *Rehoboam Rebuking the Elders* (Plate 48), *Samuel and Saul* was not painted in the Great Council Chamber until c.1530. The story was taken from I Samuel:15. When Saul conquered the Amalekites at Jehovah's command he did not destroy the whole people as he had been told to do and was therefore dethroned by Samuel. The composition of this design recalls those of Holbein's two *Triumphs* painted in London very shortly afterwards (Plate 58 and see fig. 5); like them, the ultimate source of *Samuel and Saul* was Mantegna's *Triumph of Caesar* series (fig. 3), then in Mantua.

50 *Hans of Antwerp*
WINDSOR CASTLE, Royal Collection. 1532. Oil on panel 61 × 46·8 cm. Inscribed and dated: Anno Dns [sic] 1532 auf 26 July Aetatis...

The sitter in this portrait can almost certainly be identified as Hans of Antwerp, a member of the German community in London (Plates VI, 1, 51, 52 and 55–57), who, according to the inscribed tablet on the table, sat to Holbein on 26 July 1532. If this identification is correct, it provides the first evidence of the date of Holbein's return to England, for it was presumably painted in London. Hans of Antwerp, also known as John van der Gow, settled in London in 1513 and between 1537 and 1547 received payments from the crown for goldsmith's work, including collaboration with Holbein on various projects for jewellery and metalwork (Plate 96). Hans of Antwerp was one of the witnesses to the painter's will in 1543.

51 *Georg Gisze*

BERLIN, Staatliche Museen, Gemäldegalerie. 1532. Oil on panel 96·3 × 85·7 cm. Inscribed and
dated: GGISZE; and NVLLA SINE MERORE VOLVPTAS; and Imagine Georgii Gysenii Ista
refert vultus, qua cernis, Imago Georgi Sic oculo vivos, sic habet ille genas Anno aetatis suae
XXXIIII Anno dom. 1532.

Georg Gisze was another member of the German steelyard and belonged to a family based in
Cologne. This portrait was used as a showpiece for Holbein's brilliant technique and for the
depiction of a wide variety of different materials.

52 *Derich Tybis*
VIENNA, Kunsthistorisches Museum. 1533. Oil on panel
48 × 35 cm.

The sitter is identified as another member of the German
merchant community on inscriptions within the composition. As in the case of *Hillebrandt Wedigh* (Plate 57),
Derich Tybis's pose is frontal.

(*opposite*)
VI *Derich Born*
WINDSOR CASTLE, Royal Collection. 1533. Oil on panel 60·3 × 45 cm. Inscribed: DERICHVS SI
VOCEM ADDAS IPSISSIMVS HIC SIT/HVNC DVBITES PICTOR FECERIT AN GENI-
TOR; and DER BORN ETATIS SVAE 23 ANNO 1533.

The sitter was one of several members of the German steelyard in London to be portrayed by
Holbein (Plates 50–52 and 55–57) during the months after his return to England from Basel in
1532. Born, originally from Cologne, was apparently resident in London throughout the 1530s and
1540s and in 1536 supplied war materials for the suppression of the rebellion in the north, the so-
called Pilgrimage of Grace. Another smaller portrait of him by Holbein, also painted c.1533, is in
the Alte Pinakothek in Munich (Plate 55). The Windsor portrait is inscribed with the date 1533
and the sitter's age, twenty-three, at the end of an elegiac couplet which reads in translation: 'Here
is Derich himself; add voice and you might doubt if the painter or his father created him'.

(*page 62*)
VII *Christina of Denmark, Duchess of Milan*
LONDON, National Gallery. 1538. Oil on panel 179 × 82·5 cm.

Christina of Denmark, daughter of Christian II, deposed King of Denmark, niece of Charles V,
Holy Roman Emperor, and widow of Francesco Maria Sforza, Duke of Milan, hence her mourning
dress, was one of the many princesses whose hand was sought in marriage by Henry VIII following
the death of Queen Jane Seymour in 1537. Negotiations for the match continued throughout 1538
and part of 1539, at which time Christina was living at the court of her aunt, Mary of Hungary,
Regent of the Netherlands, in Brussels. Holbein was sent to Brussels to paint her in the spring of
1538 and on 12 March Christina sat to the painter for 'thre owers space'; the English ambassador
to Brussels considered the result 'very perffight'. The study made at this one sitting was presumably
either a drawing or a painting on paper or parchment, as was the case with the portrait of *Anne of
Cleves* (Plate 72) which Holbein executed in 1539; in such a form it could be easily transported
back to England. The likeness made in Brussels was shown to Henry VIII in England on 18 March
and 'singularly pleased the King, so much so, that since he saw it he has been in much better
humor than he ever was making musicians play on their instruments all day long'. However, the
negotiations fell through and in 1541 Christina, a renowned beauty, married François, duc de Bar,
the future Duke of Lorraine, as her second husband.

DERICHVS · SI · VOCEM · ADDAS · IPSISSIMVS · HIC · SIT
HVNC · DVBITES · PICTOR · FECERIT · AN · GENITOR
DER · BORN · ETATIS · SVÆ · 23 · ANNO · 1533

53 *Jean de Dinteville and Georges de Selve ('The Ambassadors')*, detail of Plate IX.

(page 63)
VIII *The Meyer Madonna*
DARMSTADT, Schlossmuseum. Oil on panel 146·5 × 102 cm.

This altarpiece was commissioned for the chapel of the Castle of Guldendingen near Basel by Jakob Meyer whom Holbein had portrayed in 1516 (Plate 3). It is curious in showing Meyer's two wives, the first of whom had died in 1511; it also depicts his two young sons, who both died in 1526, the year in which Holbein may have begun work on this painting. X-rays have revealed that the artist made various alterations to the picture at an advanced stage, and the inclusion of Meyer's first wife may, therefore have been an afterthought. The head of the daughter, Anna, was also altered. It has been suggested that these changes were made on Holbein's return to Basel from England in 1528. Preparatory studies exist for some of the heads. There are numerous Italian features in this altarpiece, from the composition itself, which follows the *Madonna della Misericordia* type, and the use of *sfumato* in the modelling, to the beautifully foreshortened arm of the Christ Child, which must surely be related to the Virgin's stance in Leonardo's painting of *The Virgin of the Rocks* (fig. 6).

(opposite)
IX *Jean de Dinteville and Georges de Selve ('The Ambassadors')*
LONDON, National Gallery. 1533. Oil on panel 207 × 209·5 cm. Signed and dated: 1533; inscribed with the sitters' ages [twenty-nine and twenty-five respectively].

This magnificent double portrait represents the French ambassador to London, Jean de Dinteville, seigneur de Polisy, with his friend Georges de Selve, Bishop of Lavaur, who visited him in London in 1533, at the time this portrait was painted. The exact date of the painting, 11 April 1533, can be worked out from the various instruments on the buffet between the two sitters. There are many other points of interest in this picture, including the pavement, which is a virtual copy of that in the sanctuary of Westminster Abbey, and the curiously foreshortened skull in the foreground, which is one of many *vanitas* symbols in the painting. The contents of the open books can still be easily read: one is a hymn book and the other a book of arithmetic. The terrestrial globe is marked with several additional locations in France, including Polisy, which would have been relevant to the sitters. Our understanding of this picture has been greatly aided by the exposition of it by Mary Hervey published in 1900.

54 *Jean de Dinteville and Georges de Selve ('The Ambassadors')*, detail of Plate IX.

55 *Derich Born*
MUNICH, Alte Pinakothek. Watercolour on card applied to panel 10·2 cm. (diameter). Inscribed and dated (fragmentary): DE BOR/TATIS SVAE 2/MD XXX.

Born's age appears to be very close to that in the large painting of him (Plate VI), dated 1533.

ANNO.1532.

ÆTATIS.SVÆ.29.

56 *A Member of the Wedigh Family*
NEW YORK, Metropolitan Museum of Art (bequest of Edward S. Harkness). 1532. Oil on panel
41·9 × 31·8 cm. Signed with monogram and inscribed and dated: ANNO 1532. AETATIS SVAE
26; and HER. WID.

The arms of the Wedigh family of Cologne are on the sitter's signet ring; several members of the
family, Hillebrandt Wedigh (Plate 57), for instance, belonged to the German steelyard in London
for which Holbein did much work in the early 1530s.

57 *Hillebrandt Wedigh*
BERLIN, Staatliche Museen, Gemäldegalerie. 1533. Oil on panel 39 × 30 cm. Inscribed and dated:
ANNO 1533 AETATIS SVAE 39.

The sitter is shown in an unusual frontal pose rarely used in portraiture, but seen in Dürer's *Self-portrait* of 1500 (Munich, Alte Pinakothek) and later in Holbein's royal portraits, for instance those of *Christina of Denmark* (Plate VII), *Anne of Cleves* (Plate 72) and *Edward, Prince of Wales* (Plate 73).

58 *The Triumph of Riches*

PARIS, Musée du Louvre, Cabinet des Dessins. Pen and wash heightened with white 25 × 56·9 cm.

This is Holbein's finished design for one of the two *Triumphs* painted for the Guildhall of the German steelyard, c.1532–33 (see also fig. 5). Not all the figures are identified in this drawing but the names are given on later copies. The procession is centred around Plutus, who is bowed down by the burden of rich living, with his feet resting on a sack of gold, and who is seated in a magnificent chariot drawn by four white horses. Blindfolded Fortune sits immediately in front of him and scatters gold among the crowd while Ratio holds the two reins, labelled Notitia and Voluntas, which guide the horses. The horses are entitled Impostura, Contractus, Avaritia and Usura and are led by fine women called Bona Fides, Iustitia, Liberalitas and Aequalitas. This central group is surrounded by many of the famous men of fortune recorded in antiquity, while Croesus rides behind and Nemesis hovers above them all in the clouds. The meaning of this scene is clear: the instability of fortune and glory and the dangers of undue arrogance in prosperity. Such sentiments were complemented by those in *The Triumph of Poverty*, which is now known only through later copies (fig. 5).

59 *Parnassus*

BERLIN, Staatliche Museen, Kupferstichkabinett. 1533. Pen and black ink and watercolour on brown prepared paper 42·1 × 38·4 cm.

The content of this drawing showing Apollo and the Muses, as if on Parnassus, raised above a triumphal arch, connects it with the form of the triumphal arch erected by the German community in London for Queen Anne Boleyn's coronation procession on 31 May 1533.

ROBERTVS CHESEMAN . ANNO . DM .

. ETATIS . SVÆ . XLVIII ·
M · D . XXXIII ·

60 *Robert Cheseman*
THE HAGUE, Mauritshuis. 1533. Oil on panel 59 × 62·5 cm. Inscribed and dated: ROBERTVS
CHESEMAN. ETATIS.SVAE.XLVIII.ANNO DM.M.D.XXXIII.

Cheseman, who came from a distinguished line of landed gentry, is here shown holding a hooded
hawk on his gloved hand. The oblong format of this portrait is unusual and very striking.

(*opposite*)
61 *Thomas Cromwell*
NEW YORK, Frick Collection. 1533. Oil on panel 76 × 61 cm.

The date of this portrait, which is the best of several versions of a lost original by Holbein, is
determined on the basis of the letter on the table in front of Cromwell, addressed by the king 'to
our trusty and right well beloved counsillor Thomas Cromwell, Master of our Jewelhouse', to
which office Cromwell was appointed in 1533. The commission to paint Cromwell may have been
Holbein's stepping stone to employment by the court. Cromwell rose from humble origins in
Putney to high royal favour during the 1520s, and by the time of Holbein's return to England in
1532 he had become a privy councillor. In 1533 he became Chancellor of the Exchequer and then
the King's Secretary and Master of the Rolls. In 1540 he was, however, indicted for treason and
executed, as he was regarded as the chief advocate of a Protestant policy and of Henry VIII's
marriage to Anne of Cleves (Plate 72).

62 *Unknown Man with a Lute*
BERLIN, Staatliche Museen, Gemäldegalerie. Oil on panel 43·5 × 43·5 cm.

The man here portrayed was presumably a musician at the English court, for the painting is similar in style to pictures dated c.1535–36, for instance the portrait of *Richard Southwell* (Plate 70).

(*opposite*)
X *Sir Henry Guildford*
WINDSOR CASTLE, Royal Collection. 1527. Oil on panel 81·4 × 66 cm. Inscribed (at a later date): Anno D: MCCCCCXXVII Etatis Suæ XL. IX.

This portrait is one of the few datable works from Holbein's first English visit, and it was painted as a pendant to the portrait of *Lady Guildford* now in St. Louis (Plate 37). A preparatory drawing for the head in this painting is also at Windsor (Plate 38). Guildford held several high offices in the household of King Henry VIII, including that of comptroller, as indicated by the staff held by him in this portrait. His services were rewarded when he was elected a Knight of the Garter in 1526: he is shown wearing the collar of that Order in this portrait. The evidence concerning the sitter's age as given in this inscription is contradicted by Guildford's declaration that his age was forty in 1529.

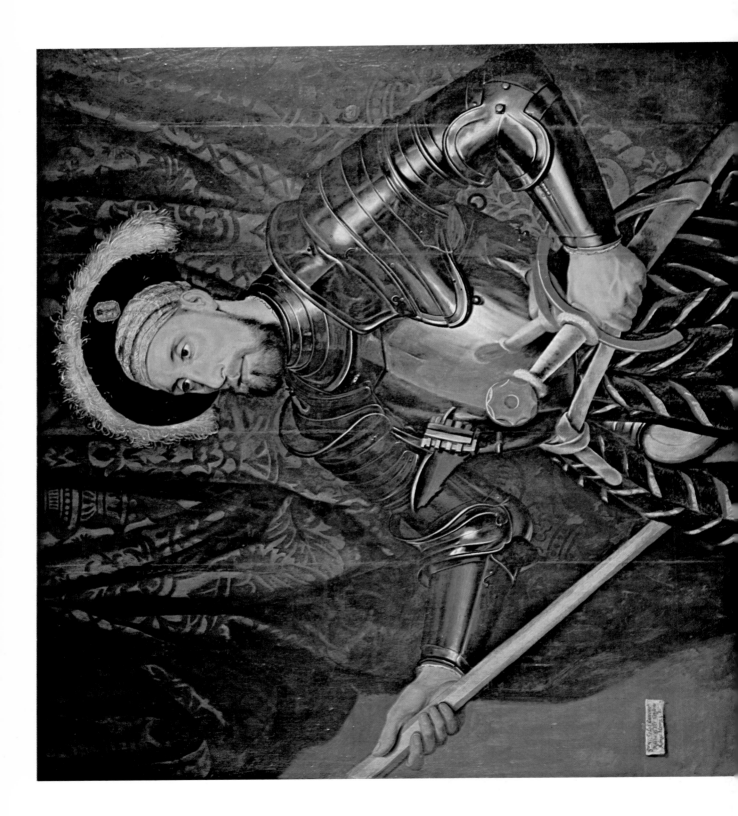

63 *Thomas Howard, third Duke of Norfolk*
WINDSOR CASTLE, Royal Collection. 1539. Oil on panel
80·3 × 61·6 cm.

In the inscription, only dimly visible today beneath layers
of overpaint, the sitter is identified as the Duke of Norfolk
and is said to be shown in his sixty-sixth year, which
would mean that the portrait was painted in 1539.
Norfolk is depicted clasping the white wand of Lord
Treasurer and the gold baton of Earl Marshal, offices he
occupied from 1522 and 1533 to 1547 respectively. He
was closely connected to the throne, for his first wife was
a daughter of King Edward IV, and he was uncle to both
Anne Boleyn and Catherine Howard, godfather to Prince
Edward and father-in-law to Henry Fitzroy, illegitimate
son of Henry VIII. However, in 1547 he was charged
with high treason and attainted; he remained in prison
under Edward VI but was fully restored by Queen
Mary I.

(*opposite*)
XI *Sir Nicholas Carew*
DUMFRIESSHIRE, Drumlanrig Castle, collection of the Duke of Buccleuch. Oil on panel
91·3 × 101·7 cm. Inscribed (at a later date): Sir Nicholas Carewe Master of the Horse to King
Henry y 8.

This striking portrait has caused problems in dating for while the preparatory drawing for the head
at Basel (Plate 45) is in black and coloured chalks, as are the studies from Holbein's first English
period, the format of the painted portrait can be connected with others, for instance, that of the
Sieur de Morette (Plate 65) executed during the 1530s, at the time of Holbein's return to England.
The drawing was followed by the painting only so far as the head was concerned, and the stance of
the figure was altered to a much bolder and more angular pose. It therefore seems that Carew may
have sat to Holbein at the end of the first visit, and that the painting was not executed until the
artist's return to England about four years later.

64 *Charles de Solier, Sieur de Morette*
DRESDEN, Staatliche Gemäldegalerie, Kupferstichkabinett. 1534–35. Black and coloured chalks and ink applied with pen and brush on pink prepared paper 33 × 24·3 cm.

The sitter was resident in England as French ambassador from 1534 to 1535. The brilliantly depicted facial features of the drawing were slightly modified for the painting, which relies for its effect instead on the overall mass of the sitter, with his thickly padded sleeves and jacket, placed in front of the richly patterned curtains.

65 *Charles de Solier, Sieur de Morette*
DRESDEN, Staatliche Gemäldegalerie. 1534–35. Oil on panel 92·5 × 78 cm.

66 *Simon George*
WINDSOR CASTLE, Royal Library. Black and coloured chalks and black ink applied with pen and brush on pink prepared paper 28·1 × 19·3 cm.

The painting (Plate 67) repeats the drawing in all essentials, but shows the sitter fully bearded. Little is known about Simon George except that he came from a Dorset family and settled at Quotoule in Cornwall.

67 *Simon George*

FRANKFURT, Städelsches Kunstinstitut. Oil on panel 31 cm. (diameter).

ANNO · DÑI · 1541 ·   ETATIS · SVÆ · 28 ·

(opposite)
68 *Unknown Man*
VIENNA, Kunsthistorisches Museum. 1541. Oil on panel 47 × 35 cm. Inscribed and dated: ANNO. DNI.1541 ETATIS SVAE 28.

The identity of the sitter is unknown but the date inscribed across the background establishes that he was resident in England. His pose is a curious amalgam of those of the two members of the Wedigh family (Plates 56 and 57), whose portraits Holbein had painted about ten years earlier.

(above left)
69 *Sir Richard Southwell*
WINDSOR CASTLE, Royal Library. 1536. Black and coloured chalks with ink applied with pen and brush on pink prepared paper 37 × 28·1 cm. Inscribed: ANNO ETTATIS SVAE 33; and Die augen ein wenig gelbatt.

This drawing is a preparatory study for the Uffizi portrait (Plate 70), which followed it exactly.

(above right)
70 *Sir Richard Southwell*
FLORENCE, Galleria degli Uffizi. 1536. Oil on panel 47·5 × 38 cm. Inscribed and dated: X° IVLII ANNO H.VIII XXVIII° ETATIS SVAE.ANNO XXXIII.

From the inscription, which states that the portrait was painted in the twenty-eighth year of Henry VIII's reign, we can calculate its date as 1536. At that time Southwell was acting as an agent for Thomas Cromwell in the dissolution of the monasteries; he was at various times sheriff and Member of Parliament for Norfolk and was knighted in 1542. The preparatory study for this portrait is at Windsor (Plate 69); both the drawing and the painting are meticulous in showing the scars on Southwell's forehead and neck, which, in the case of the drawing, were formerly thought to be old repairs in the paper. The drawing is annotated: 'the eyes a little yellowish'. This painting was given by Thomas Howard, second Earl of Arundel, the great connoisseur and collector, who had a particular interest in Holbein, to Cosimo II, Grand Duke of Tuscany.

(overleaf)
71 *King Henry VIII*
LONDON, National Portrait Gallery. c.1536–37. Black ink and watercolour washes on paper mounted on canvas 257·8 × 137·1 cm.

This is part of Holbein's original cartoon for his wall painting in the Privy Chamber of Whitehall Palace, executed c.1536–37. Although the painting was destroyed in 1698 it is known from copies by Leemput (fig. 9). The creation of the magnificent, even overwhelming, image of the king was one of Holbein's great achievements during his stay in England; the contrast between Henry VIII in the foreground and the graceful but almost slight figure of his father, Henry VII, behind is especially marked. The cartoon for the king's head, which is close to that in the Thyssen portrait (Plate XII), is on a separate sheet of paper, cut out and stuck onto the whole.

72 *Anne of Cleves*
PARIS, Musée du Louvre. 1539. Tempera on parchment worked over in oil and laid down on panel 65 × 48 cm.

The circumstances surrounding the painting of the portrait of *Anne of Cleves* were similar to those for *Christina of Denmark* (Plate VII). Holbein was sent to Düren to paint the two sisters of the Duke of Cleves in June 1539. The unusual technique of the Louvre portrait was probably determined by the need to transport it easily back to England. Henry VIII was evidently sufficiently satisfied with Anne's appearance to agree to the marriage scheme, and in January 1540 he married her.
However, the union lasted only six months as the king came to be repulsed by his consort, 'the Flanders mare', and following the divorce she lived with her own court at Richmond.

PARVVLE PATRISSA, PATRIÆ VIRTVTIS ET HÆRES
    ESTO, NIHIL MAIVS MAXIMVS ORBIS HABET.
GNATVM VIX POSSVNT COELVM ET NATVRA DEDISSE,
    HVIVS QVEM PATRIS, VICTVS HONORET HONOS.
ÆQVATO TANTVM, TANTI TV FACTA PARENTIS,
    VOTA HOMINVM, VIX QVO PROGREDIANTVR, HABENT
VINCITO, VICISTI. QVOT REGES PRISCVS ADORAT
    ORBIS, NEC TE QVI VINCERE POSSIT, ERIT.

73 *Edward, Prince of Wales*
WASHINGTON, National Gallery of Art (Andrew Mellon collection). 1539. Oil on panel 57 × 44 cm.

This picture is normally identified with the gift presented to the king by the artist on New Year's Day 1540: 'By Hanse Holbeyne a Table of the pictour of the prince [prince's] grace'. Below the portrait are Latin distychs composed by the court poet Richard Morysin, encouraging the prince to surpass his father's achievements.

(above)
74 *Edward, Prince of Wales, with a Monkey*
BASEL, Offentliche Kunstsammlung, Kupferstichkabinett. c.1543. Black and coloured chalks with ink applied with brush and watercolour 40·1 × 30·9 cm.

This curious drawing must have been executed in Holbein's last years and therefore provides a good example of the recurrence of similar techniques at widely separated intervals throughout his career; in many respects it is very similar to the drawing of *John Godsalve* at Windsor (Plate 39), which is datable to c.1528.

The Lady Eliot.

(*above left*)
76 *William Reskimer*
WINDSOR CASTLE, Royal Library. Black and coloured chalks on pink prepared paper 29·3 × 21·2 cm.

William Reskimer was a member of an ancient Cornish family and was first recorded as being at court in 1525 when he became Page of the Chamber; he continued to hold this office throughout the 1530s, and in 1546 he was appointed a Gentleman Usher. He had died by 1564. The use of coloured chalks by Holbein suggests that the drawing, a study for a painting in the Royal Collection, is probably datable to c.1532–33.

(*above right*)
77 *Sir Thomas Elyot*
WINDSOR CASTLE, Royal Library. Black and coloured chalks reinforced with black ink and body colour on pink prepared paper 28·6 × 20·6 cm.

(*opposite*)
75 *Margaret à Barrow, Lady Elyot*
WINDSOR CASTLE, Royal Library. Black and coloured chalks reinforced with black ink and body colour on pink prepared paper 28 × 20·9 cm.

Thomas Elyot was a member of a Wiltshire landowning family and after studying law at Oxford and in London he became Clerk to the King's Council; he married Margaret à Barrow in 1522. Elyot was knighted in 1530 and in the following year published *The boke named the Governour* in which he wrote of his 'blessed and stable' friendship with Thomas More, although he later asked Cromwell to forget this and to affirm his loyalty to the king. As with the portrait of *William Reskimer* (Plate 76), this pair of drawings, which are apparently not connected with any known paintings, should probably be dated c.1532–33.

78 *Unknown Man*

WINDSOR CASTLE, Royal Library. Black and red chalk and black ink applied with pen and brush on pink prepared paper 27·5 × 21·1 cm. Inscribed: atlass; and at [silk]; and S [?satin].

As with the portrait of *Thomas Boleyn* (Plate 44) and *John More the younger* (Plate 32), this drawing is remarkable for the freedom in the handling of the brushwork of the draperies and for the meticulous penwork in the facial features.

79 *Unknown Man*
WINDSOR CASTLE, Royal Library. Black and coloured chalks and black ink on pink prepared paper
29·8 × 22·2 cm.

Although the identity of the sitter is unknown, the date of the drawing can be ascertained on the
basis of its connection with the small circular oil painting in the Metropolitan Museum of Art,
New York, which gives the sitter's age as twenty-eight and the date as 1535. The drawing has
evidently been trimmed on both sides and at the bottom, for the miniature includes the sitter's
hands and other features missing from the drawing.

(above right)
81 *Nicholas Bourbon*
WINDSOR CASTLE, Royal Library. 1535. Black and coloured chalks and pen and black ink 30·9 × 26 cm.

Bourbon was a French poet, born in 1503, who came to England in 1535. In the following year he wrote to the King's Secretary, Thomas Solimar, asking to be remembered to his many friends in England, including 'Mr. Hans the royal painter, the Apelles of our time'. The pure profile is seldom encountered in Holbein's portraits, although a memorable example of its use is the Louvre *Erasmus* (Plate 26).

(above left)
80 *John Poyntz*
WINDSOR CASTLE, Royal Library. Black and coloured chalks with pen and ink on pink prepared paper 29·5 × 23·3 cm.

The sitter was probably John Poyntz of Alderley, whose first wife Elizabeth was the sister of Henry Guildford (Plate X) and who died in 1544. He appears to wear a professional cap of some kind and is depicted in an unusually casual pose, indicating perhaps that his likeness was to have been incorporated into a group portrait.

(opposite)
XII *King Henry VIII*
LUGANO, Thyssen-Bornemisza Collection. 1536–37. Oil and tempera on panel 27·5 × 19·5 cm.

This is probably the only surviving panel painting of the king by Holbein which is entirely autograph. The king's appearance and pose are closely connected with those in the Whitehall cartoon (Plate 71), painted c.1536–37. The Thyssen portrait may be one side of a diptych with portraits of King Henry VIII and Queen Jane Seymour which was recorded in the royal inventories of 1542 and 1547. The gold thread of the fabric, the embroidery around the shirt neck and the gold in the chain and jewellery were all painted with real gold, as they were in the portrait of *Edward, Prince of Wales* (Plate 73). The king's face is depicted with a flatness typical of Holbein's royal portraits; it is easy to overlook the modelling in the lower part of the panel and in particular in the right hand.

(above left)
72 *Sir Philip Hoby*
WINDSOR CASTLE, Royal Library. Black and coloured chalks on pink prepared paper 30 × 22·3 cm.

Hoby was a diplomat and courtier who must have become well-known to Holbein for he accompanied the artist to Brussels in March 1538 when Holbein was despatched to draw the likeness of *Christina of Denmark* (Plate VII). He belonged to the circle of Thomas Cromwell but survived his fall from favour and was knighted in 1544. He first appeared at court holding important offices in the mid-1530s, from which time this drawing probably dates.

(above right)
73 *Scholar or Cleric*
BAKEWELL, Chatsworth House, Devonshire collection. Point of brush and black ink over black chalk on pink prepared paper 21·7 × 18·4 cm. Inscribed: HH.

This drawing probably dates from early in Holbein's second English period.

(opposite)
XIII *Queen Jane Seymour*
VIENNA, Kunsthistoriches Museum. 1536–37. Oil on panel 65 × 40·5 cm.

Jane Seymour was lady-in-waiting to both Queen Catherine of Aragon and Queen Anne Boleyn before marrying Henry VIII as his third wife in 1536, the day after Queen Anne's execution. In 1537 she bore a son, the future King Edward VI (Plates 73 and 74), but died two days after his birth. The pose in which Queen Jane is here portrayed is similar to that in the preparatory study at Windsor and in the Whitehall mural (see fig. 9), with which this painting must be contemporary. There are several other versions of this portrait the best of which is the small panel in the Mauritshuis, The Hague.

84 *Sir Thomas Wyatt*
WINDSOR CASTLE, Royal Library. Black and coloured chalks and ink applied with pen and brush on pink prepared paper 37·1 × 27 cm.

Wyatt was both poet and diplomat and one of the most colourful figures of Henry VIII's reign. His father was the courtier Sir Henry Wyatt, of whom there exists a portrait attributed to Holbein in the Louvre. In 1524 Thomas was appointed Clerk of King's Jewels. Twelve years later he was sent to the Tower, accused of having been Queen Anne Boleyn's lover before she married the king, but he was soon released. He continued to work for the court until his sudden death in 1542.

85 *Solomon and the Queen of Sheba*
WINDSOR CASTLE, Royal Library. Ink applied with pen and brush, watercolour, body colour and gold paint 22·7 × 18·3 cm. Inscribed.

The rôle of Solomon was adopted by Henry VIII in this miniature painting, and as we know that the king was bearded as early as 1519 it is now no longer necessary to date this work to c.1535, as was previously thought. Indeed the rather elongated forms of the figures, moving in graceful lines across the foreground, suggest a date late in Holbein's first English period rather than early in his second. This would, of course, presuppose Holbein's entering royal service considerably before he is documented as having worked for the king. The miniature was probably intended as a presentation piece like the Washington portrait of *Edward, Prince of Wales* (Plate 73) which was probably given to the king by the artist on New Year's Day, 1540. Although the scale and context of this painting are unique in Holbein's *oeuvre*, it is possible to find points of compositional similarity with other works, especially decorative schemes, for instance *Rehoboam Rebuking the Elders* (Plates 47 and 48), which would have been executed shortly after this miniature. The architecture is also fairly close to that in the Whitehall mural.

86 *Henry Brandon, second Duke of Suffolk*
WINDSOR CASTLE, Royal Collection. 1541. Tempera on vellum applied to a playing card 5·6 cm. (diameter). Inscribed and dated: etatis.sue.5.6.sepdem./ANNO 1535.

87 *Charles Brandon, third Duke of Suffolk*
WINDSOR CASTLE, Royal Collection. 1541. Tempera on vellum applied to a playing card 5·5 cm. (diameter). Inscribed and dated: ANN/1541/ETATIS SVAE 3/10.MARCI.

These miniatures appear to have been painted as pendants in 1541, so that the date on the portrait of the second duke must record the elder boy's birth rather than the date of the miniature's execution. These miniatures were in the collection of King Charles I, when they were stated to have been 'Don by Hanc Holben'. Their exquisite technique confirms this attribution. The Brandon boys were closely connected to the court: they were the sons of the fourth marriage of Henry VIII's trusted friend and devoted servant, Charles Brandon, first Duke of Suffolk, whose third wife had been the king's own sister, Mary Tudor, the dowager Queen of France. This meant that the Brandon boys' half-sisters, Frances and Eleanor Brandon, were nieces to Henry VIII and first cousins and, in some eyes, heiresses to Edward VI, with whom Henry Brandon (Plate 86) was educated and at whose coronation he carried the Orb. Both Henry and Charles Brandon attended St. John's College, Cambridge, and were renowned for their learning; they died of the sweating sickness within half an hour of each other in 1551.

88 *Lady Audley*
WINDSOR CASTLE, Royal Collection. Tempera on vellum applied to a playing card 5·6 cm. (diameter).

This likeness is connected with that shown in one of Holbein's drawings, also in the Royal Collection, inscribed 'The Lady Audley'. There were two families called Audley at court and it is probable that the lady portrayed in this miniature was Elizabeth, the daughter of the second Marquess of Dorset, who married the Lord Chancellor, Lord Audley of Walden, in 1538 as his second wife. After his death in 1544 she remarried; she died before 1564. Both drawing and miniature are probably datable to c.1540.

89 *A Lady called 'Catherine Howard'*
WINDSOR CASTLE, Royal Collection. Tempera on vellum applied to a playing card 6·3 cm. (diameter).

From the 1840s this miniature has been described as a portrait of Queen Catherine Howard, but there is no authentic likeness of Henry VIII's fifth consort. There is another version of this miniature in the collection of the Duke of Buccleuch.

90 *Mrs. Pemberton*
LONDON, Victoria and Albert Museum. Watercolour on a playing card 5·4 cm. (diameter).

This miniature is set as a locket in an enamelled gold frame which bears on the reverse the arms of the Sago di Lago family quartered with those of Pemberton. The woman represented is probably, therefore, Margaret Pemberton (d.1576), daughter of Richard Throgmorton and wife of Robert Pemberton, whose paternal grandmother was the last heir of the Sago di Lago family.

91 *Self-portrait*
DUMFRIESSHIRE, Drumlanrig Castle, collection of the Duke of Buccleuch. 1543. Watercolour on card 3·7 cm. (diameter).

This is one of four versions of a miniature self-portrait of Holbein, three of which are inscribed with the sitter's age and the date of his death, 1543. In each of these the artist is shown in the act of painting himself.

93 *William Roper*
NEW YORK, Metropolitan Museum of Art (Rogers fund). 1536-40? Watercolour on card 4·5 cm. (diameter).

Margaret, the eldest and best-loved of Thomas More's children, married William Roper, a long-standing member of More's household, in 1521. At the time she was sixteen and he was in his twenties; this pair of miniatures show the sitters about seventeen years later, a few years after More's death. It is not possible to arrive at a precise date owing to the conflicting evidence provided by the sitter's ages given on these miniatures and elsewhere. Roper came from a wealthy Kentish family and like Sir John and Sir Thomas More was a member of Lincoln's Inn. In around 1518 he entered More's household and remained 'xvj yeares and more in house conversant with him', despite his early adoption of the Lutheran faith. Margaret Roper, a highly intelligent and devout woman, predeceased her husband by over thirty years and was the mother of five children. This pair of miniatures is tentatively attributed to Holbein by most scholars, but the hand seems slightly different to that seen in the artist's other miniatures (Plates 86-91).

86

87

88

89

90

91

92

93

4 King Henry VIII Granting the Charter to the Barber-Surgeon's Company
LONDON, Barber-Surgeon's Hall, Worshipful Company of Barbers. Oil and tempera on canvas
180·3 × 312·4 cm.

This painting was commissioned in 1541 following the unification of the barbers' and surgeons'
guilds; the president of the newly-formed body is seen taking the charter from the king, who is
raised above the ranks of barbers and surgeons. Two of the latter were portrayed by Holbein in
separate portraits, *John Chambers* (Vienna, Kunsthistorisches Museum) and *Sir William Butts* (Boston,
Isabella Stewart Gardner Museum). This rather unsatisfactory painting was apparently left
unfinished by Holbein at his death and was therefore completed by members of his studio. Another
version of the composition belongs to the Royal College of Surgeons, London, and X-rays suggest
that it is Holbein's original cartoon covered by layers of later paint. The king appears in this
composition almost as an icon, untouchable and raised above the other particiipants in the scene; in
addition he is painted on a slightly larger scale.

(opposite)
Design For Queen Jane Seymour's Cup
LONDON, British Museum, Department of Prints and Drawings. 1536–37. Pen and ink and wash
7·3 × 14·3 cm.

The abundance of love-knots linking the initials 'H' and 'I' and the many appearances of Jane
Seymour's motto, 'Bound to Obey and Serve', prove beyond doubt that this design was intended
for a cup closely connected to Henry VIII and his third consort. The actual piece was described as
in the Royal Collection in 1625 when King Charles I sent Buckingham to Holland to sell it,
together with various other treasures of a similar nature. 'Item a faire standing Cupp of Goulde,
furnished about the cover with eleaven Dyamonds, and two poynted Dyamonds about the Cupp,
seaventeene Table Dyamonds and one Pearle Pendant upon the Cupp, with theis words: BOUND
TO OBEY AND SERVE and H and I knitt together; in the Topp of the Cover the Queenes
Armes and Queene Janes Armes houlden by twoe Boyes under a Crowne Imperiall, weighing
threescore and five ounces and a half.' The right side of the design was completed by a later hand.

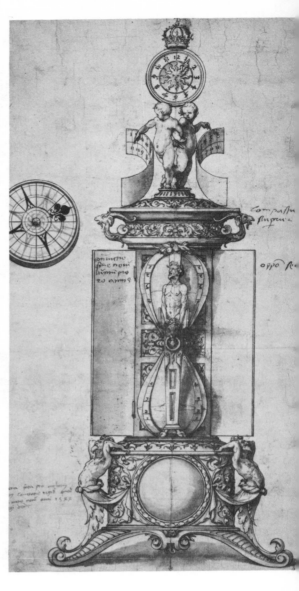

(above left)
96 *Design for Hans of Antwerp's Cup*
BASEL, Öffentliche Kunstsammlung, Kupferstichkabinett. Pen and ink with wash and black chalk
25·1 × 16 cm.

Holbein only drew the left side of this design; the right side is a counter-proof. Around the edges of
the lid of this cup is inscribed the name of Hans of Antwerp who was a close friend of Holbein
(Plate 50). At the artist's death Hans of Antwerp acted as executor of the will, which reveals that
Holbein had some debts outstanding with Hans.

(above right)
97 *Design for Sir Anthony Denny's Clock*
LONDON, British Museum, Department of Prints and Drawings. 1543. Pen and wash
41·1 × 21·3 cm. Inscribed with directions by the artist and by Denny: Strena facta pro anthony
deny camerario regio quod in initio novi anni 1544 regi dedit.

According to the inscription, the clock made from this design was presented by Denny, at the time
Chamberlain to the Household, to King Henry VIII as a New Year's gift in 1544. Holbein's design
is for an hour-glass enclosed within an elaborately decorated case, which is itself surmounted by
putti holding curved strips, which serve as sundials, and supporting a clock; the whole structure is
surmounted by a crown. The figures of terms and the decorative language used in this drawing are
typical of Mannerist designs made throughout Europe, but especially in Germany, around the
middle of the sixteenth century.

(*above left*)
98 *Design for a Parade Dagger*
LONDON, British Museum, Department of Prints and Drawings. Pen and ink and wash 45·4 × 12·4
cm.

This very ornate design must surely have been intended for a royal commission. The dagger was
evidently to be studded with jewels, in the areas which Holbein left blank.

(*above right*)
99 *Design for a Centrepiece*
BASEL, Öffentliche Kunstsammlung, Kupferstichkabinett. Pen and ink 17·4 × 40 cm.

This design, from a group of studies for objects all apparently destined for the king, appears to
have been for an elaborate table decoration, with three superimposed basins and numerous satyrs
and classical scenes, surmounted by the figure of Jupiter brandishing a thunderbolt. It is among
Holbein's most ornate designs for the decorative arts.

100 *Design for a Chimneypiece*
LONDON, British Museum, Department of Prints and Drawings. 1540. Pen with coloured washes
54 × 42·7 cm.

This elaborate design was probably intended for Bridewell Palace; it is rich in royal and Tudor
emblems and complex symbolism. In the different divisions formed by the columns, friezes and
terms there are two scenes of combat. This is one of the few surviving sheets of designs by Holbein
for items of internal decoration, as opposed to mural paintings.

101 *'Scaevola and Porsena' Title-page*

LONDON, British Library. 1516. Woodcut 18·3 × 12 cm. Signed with monogram.

This title-page was first used in Gazaeus Aeneas's *De immortalitate animae*, published by Froben (Plate 12) in Basel in 1516, but was re-used two years later for Thomas More's *Epigrammata* and Erasmus's *Encomium Matrimonii*, both also published by Froben, as well as elsewhere. The lower part of the page shows the story of Gaius Mucius, a young Roman nobleman who tried to rid his country of the Etruscans, led by their king, Lars Porsena. He entered the king's tent, shown bottom right, but mistakenly stabbed Porsena's secretary rather than Porsena himself. Gaius Mucius was promptly arrested and condemned to death, but he so impressed his captors by his bravery when he thrust his right hand into a fire in the Etruscan camp that he was freed. He thereafter received the title 'Scaevola', 'the left-handed'. At this stage of his career Holbein simply provided the printer with his designs, which were then translated onto wood and metal blocks by one of the printer's craftsmen; the result is crude when compared with the later designs cut by Hans Lutzelberger (Plates 102, 103 and 105–108).

102 *Illustration to the Opening Page of St. Matthew's Gospel*

LONDON, British Library. 1523. Woodcut 8·2 × 6·6 cm.

This exquisite vignette, first published in Adam Petri's *New Testament* (Christmond, 1522), was among the first of Holbein's designs to be cut on the wood-block by Hans Lutzelberger. From this point, Holbein actually sketched his design for a woodcut onto the block before handing it over to Lutzelberger to cut it. The quality of the woodcuts made by Lutzelberger is superb.

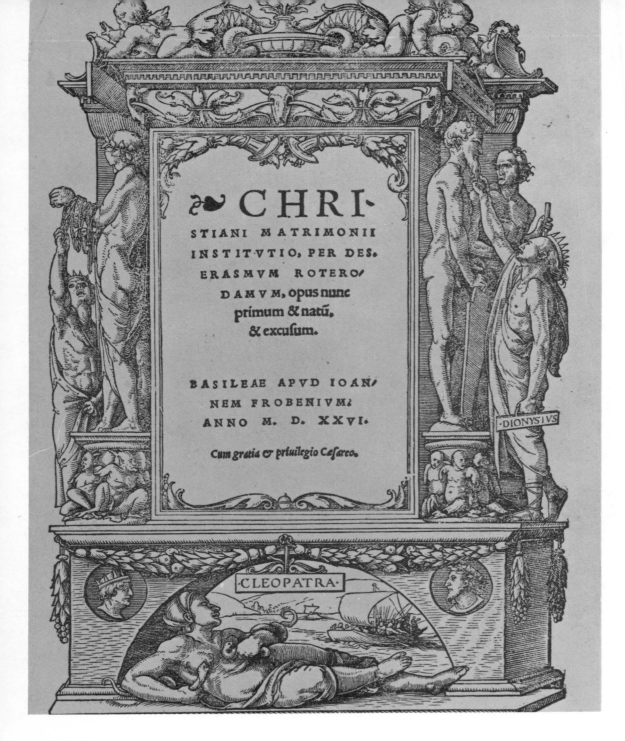

103 'Cleopatra' Title-page
LONDON, British Museum, Department of Prints and Drawings. 1526. Woodcut 23·7 × 16 cm.

This title-page, cut by Lutzelberger, was first used in Erasmus's *Divi Hilarii Pictavorum Episcopi Lucubrationes* published by Froben in Basel in 1523. It was frequently used in later books, and this plate is taken from the 1526 edition of Erasmus's *Christiani Matrimonii Institutio*. It is an obvious example of Italian influence and is therefore typical of Holbein's work in all genre in the early 1520s. The title page derives its name from the reclining figure of Cleopatra.

(opposite)
104 The Coverdale Bible Title-page
LONDON, British Library. 1535. Woodcut 31·5 × 18·2 cm.

Holbein's woodcut for the title-page of the Coverdale Bible, the first complete edition of the Bible in English, was in four separate blocks. In the lower strip Henry VIII appears enthroned, sword in hand, delivering the Word to the lords spiritual while the lords temporal attend. David and St. Paul stand at either side, representing the Old and New Testaments. The composition of this scene is, in general terms, similar to that of *Rehoboam Rebuking the Elders* and *Solomon and the Queen of Sheba* (Plates 47 and 85).

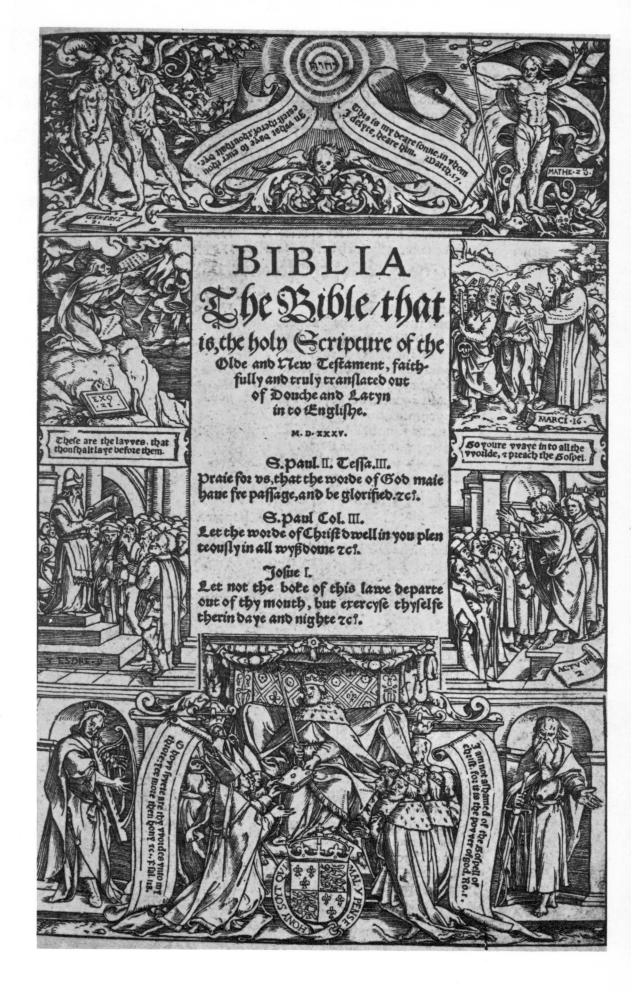

105–108 *Proofs from the Dance of Death Series*
LONDON, British Museum, Department of Prints and Drawings. Published 1538. Woodcuts 6·5 × 5 cm. (each plate).

(*top left*)
105 *The Count*

(*top centre*)
106 *The Ploughman*

(*top right*)
107 *The Last Judgement*

(*above*)
108 *The Arms of Death*

The series of *The Dance of Death* woodcuts was first published in *Les simulacres et historiées faces de la mort* (Lyon, 1538) but were mostly cut by Lutzelberger in 1523–25. The plates here illustrated show the Count, the Ploughman, the Last Judgment and the Arms of Death. The series had an immediate and widespread popularity.

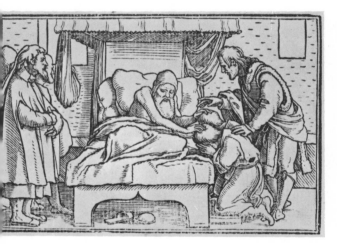

09 and 110 *Plates from 'The Old Testament' Series*
ONDON, British Library. Published 1538. Woodcuts 6 × 8 cm. (each plate).

op left)
09 *Jacob Blessing Ephraim and Manasseh*

above left)
10 *Judith and the Head of Holofernes*

These plates first appeared in the *Historiarum veteris instrumenti icones ad vivum expressae*, published in Lyon in 1538, but, as with *The Dance of Death* series (Plates 105–108), they were probably cut over en years earlier. The Old Testament scenes were issued as a picture book with ninety-one separate plates, rather than as textual illustrations in the usual way.

above right)
11 *Desiderius Erasmus*
ONDON, British Museum, Department of Prints and Drawings. 1535. Woodcut 28·6 × 14·8 cm.

This portrait of *Erasmus* is the last of a long line of likenesses of him from Holbein's hand. It is unique in this series in showing him standing full-length.

Eskimo Art

Eskimo Art

Cottie Burland

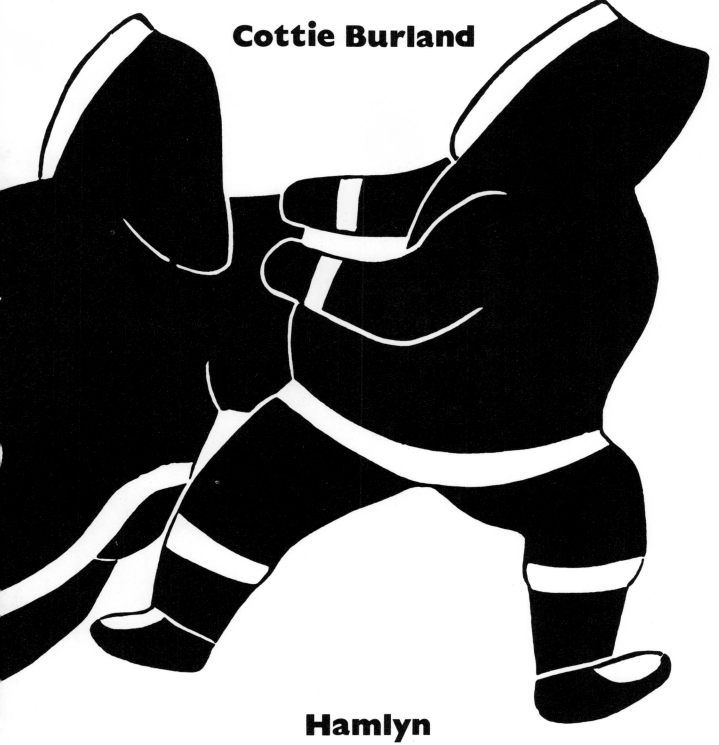

Hamlyn

London · New York · Sydney · Toronto

Published by
The Hamlyn Publishing Group Limited
London · New York · Sydney · Toronto
Hamlyn House, Feltham, Middlesex, England
© copyright The Hamlyn Publishing Group Limited 1973

ISBN 0 600 33083 4

Text set in 'Monophoto' Ehrhardt by
London Filmsetters Limited
Printed in England by
Sir Joseph Causton and Sons Limited

Contents

Foreword

No human race has won its living in a harsher environment than the hundred thousand or so hunters of the arctic ice. No people have been so richly reported, or so little understood, as these folk. Even the name given to them was a misnomer. In 1611 the word Escomminquois was used by the explorer Biard who had heard the Chippewa Indians talk of a northern group of ice hunters as Ashquimec which means, 'They eat raw flesh'. This was often true enough, but it was not the real name of those fur-clad hunters; they called themselves simply Inuit which means, 'people'. The Eskimos had been separated from most other humans for thousands of years and were justified in thinking that they were the only people on the earth.

In talking of the art of the Eskimos we are dealing with an idea which was not part of their normal life. They made many things, often of great beauty, but they were to them no more than practical objects. A snow knife or a bow drill was a tool, although sometimes its smooth surfaces were ornamented by a few scenes of hunting in order to make it lucky. Toggles were carved to resemble the heads of seals and polar bears because these were the animals desired by the hunter for his family dinner. Life was hard, and time moved uncertainly, from the rush of energy in a hunt to long hours of waiting by a seal blow-hole in the ice. In the long nights of winter when the sun was not seen for months there were moonless or stormy times when equipment was made, and sometimes the worker produced objects of astonishing artistic value, just because he was making a useful object and decorating it without any self-consciousness.

In recent years the world of the Eskimo has changed radically. New weapons for the hunter, new propulsion for boats and sledges, and new concentrations of population have meant new needs. A market has opened for the sale of Eskimo carvings; a friend came among the people to instruct them how to expand their simple graphic art into the production of beautiful lithographic prints. The natural ability of the people has made possible a new source of income. Not all Eskimos have the time or the inclination to make such works of art, and a new phenomenon has arisen in their social structure: the artist as a professional. The Eskimos now stand at a cross-roads of culture, for the old life has nearly disappeared. They know well that ancestral ways are going for ever. Many realise the value of entering a world culture with its education, trade and technology. The northland has been burst wide open for its oil and its strategic potential. Its people have not just lost heart and died, but being intelligent and capable they have faced their problems and found solutions. They have not despised the white man but have accepted offers of help and, with much reticence, have adopted new ways.

It is now a moot point whether the old ways of the Eskimos have any meaning. They may even face the day when their old world will be abandoned for a more hospitable environment. All is changing, but the children of the ancient hunters have carried on some traditions and still make beauty. However, to understand this world of the modern Eskimo artist we must make a voyage into the past, indeed to a very distant past when our own ancestors were also fighting the perils of an Ice Age.

4 Hunter returning with seal. Soapstone (12 cm high). Cut at Povungnituk, Quebec, about 1955. (Collection: Dr Helge Larsen, Copenhagen)

The First Comers

The earliest date for the presence of humans in the arctic comes from Alaska, where a cache of stone tools has been found in association with fragments of wood. The radio-carbon date given to this find is twenty-eight thousand years ago. It is highly probable that a few families were in the American continent even before then, but this is the earliest trace we have of man in the world of the far north. Conditions then were harsher than they are now. It was the height of the last glaciation, when so much ice was locked up in the enormous ice caps around the poles that the level of the oceans was nearly two hundred feet below the present sea level. It is almost impossible to understand the conditions in which a family of advanced Stone Age hunters crossed over solid land where now the waters of the Bering Strait achieve periodic liquidity. There was, in fact, no mass migration, because hunting folk cannot find enough food if they travel in groups of more than a few families. Nor were they naked savages; they must have had satisfactory garments of fur, and some means of controlling fire. A few bones from similar levels show that physically the earliest hunters were not radically different from the Eskimos of recent times.

Unfortunately, the immense period of elapsed time has destroyed all their materials except the sharp-edged blades flaked from silicious rock. But the skill of the craftsman who made the blades is without doubt. They are not relics of a truly primitive people, but of some unknown tribe whose hunters carried really efficient knives and spears, where the stone flakes had been worked around the edges by pressure flaking to give symmetry and a razor-sharp cutting edge. Those hunters in the arctic of long ago were no whit inferior in their skill with stone than their contemporaries in Europe. They were the precursors of the peoples who made the Denbigh flint culture in Alaska and whose flaked-stone tools extend far along the Canadian arctic and even to Greenland. In Canada their work is simply labelled pre-Dorset. Radio-carbon dating has given us the impression that they moved from west to east, and that they lived more than five thousand years ago. There exist a few of their bone and ivory objects, but nothing is yet reported which can be described as a work of artistic quality. The stone blades have been found in excavations near areas inhabited in recent times by the Eskimos, but so far no really good evidence about the house types and the way of life of these makers of flint tools of great efficiency has been discovered. Nevertheless, they must have had some shelters. It was in their time too that the climate began to ameliorate and the oceans to melt.

By some three thousand years ago there was a change. Whether it was a change of population, with more tribes moving in from Siberia, or simply a development by the local populace we do not know. But the Old Bering Sea culture appeared in Alaska and continued around the shores of the Arctic Ocean, where, after about two centuries, it reached Greenland. In the Arctic Ocean regions it is known as the Dorset culture, and there it differs somewhat from the Bering Strait region because of the more restricted ecology where there was little access to the open sea.

The Old Bering Sea culture left some specimens of art in ivory. Styles developed as time went on and pieces became much more rich in design, evolving towards the Ipiutak culture of Alaska where decorative art was much used in beautifying the surface of weapons and tools. The delicacy of this Alaskan art-form is exquisite, with its sweeping curves and spirals incised quite lightly over the curved surfaces of the ivory.

The characteristic dwelling of the Bering Strait people was the earth house, a pit dug in the earth, not very deep, but sufficient to allow a pool of warm air to accumulate. Around this, walls were erected, mostly of wood in the south, and in the north of whale ribs and any other large bones to be found nearby. Presumably these walls were fortified by layers of skin covered with sods of earth. From remains in the house ruins it has been deduced that the people of this early period were, like the later Eskimos, seasonal hunters. That is, they spent the summer in skin tents going after the land animals, and in the winter returned to the coastal settlements for a period of ice hunting. It is probable that around the beginning of

5 **Old wooden dance mask** with flaring nostrils typical of the Dorset culture. From Point Barrow, Alaska. Acquired in 1909. (Horniman Museum, London)

the Christian era the climate was a few degrees warmer than at present, so hunting conditions were better.

On the shores of the Arctic Ocean, life was never easy. The only wood was driftwood, moving with currents in the summer. The Dorset culture people made themselves earth houses, often round and not rectangular like the Alaskan ones. They used whale ribs as supporting beams in great numbers, and must have spent much time in whale hunting with harpoons. They left no evidence of using the single-seater kayaks of later times, but took off on hunting expeditions in large skin-covered open boats, rather like curraghs, which they called umiaks. In all their settlements so far, only one small sledge made up of bones has been found. It appears that they had no dogs, and that this small sledge must have been

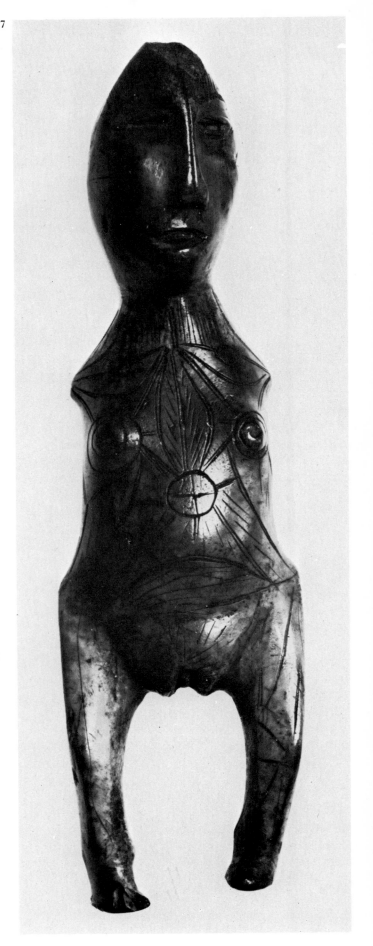

6 Head made from walrus tusk, broken off from body (8.3 cm high). From the Punuk Islands, Bering Sea. Prehistoric Okvik culture, about A.D. 0–500. (Danish National Museum, Copenhagen)

7 Armless female figure. Ivory. From the Punuk Islands, Bering Sea. Prehistoric Okvik culture, about A.D. 200. (University of Alaska Museum, College, Alaska)

8 Mask made from carved pieces of walrus tusk. The back is roughly finished and was probably nailed on to wood. Under the mouth two large pieces of jet have been inserted as labrets (lip plugs), and eighty cavities were apparently inlaid with jet. (16.4 cm high). Grave find from the Point Hope settlement, Alaska. Ipiutak culture, about A.D. 300–1000. (The American Museum of Natural History, New York)

10

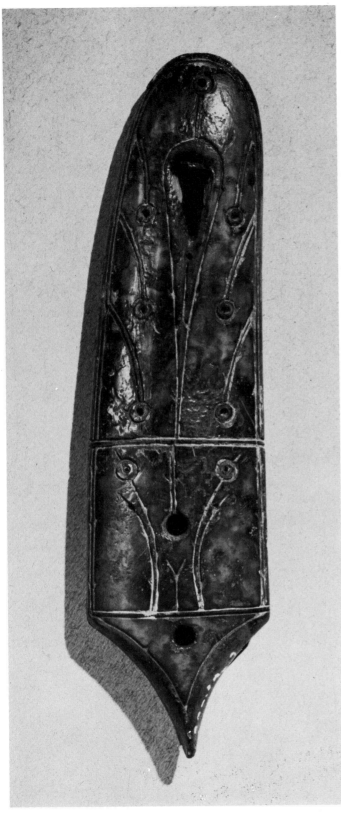

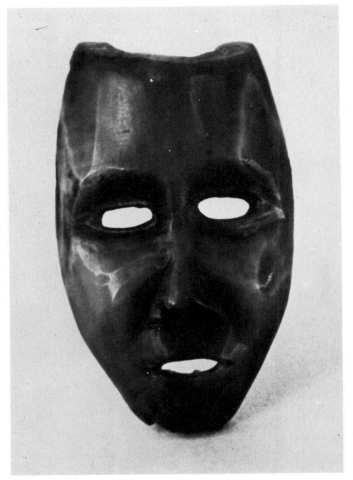

dragged by the hunter. From the limited number of excavations made in the remains of their villages it seems that most of the harvest of the hunter was carried on his back, or the backs of his wives.

The art styles of the Dorset culture are as distinct as those of the Alaskan Bering Sea and Ipiutak people. On the whole, Dorset material is strong and marked by rather coarse cutting, though the earliest known piece, a tiny ivory mask from Igloolik which has been radio-carbon dated to about 780 B.C., is a work of great delicacy and sensitivity. However, most Dorset art is marked by deep grooves across figures and masks, simple forms in the little figure carvings, and quite often an omission of arms because of the difficulty of carving such appendages. A good deal of carving in driftwood has survived. But we know nothing so far about Dorset culture clothing, except for a few lines on figures which suggest that anorak and trousers were standard, for among the Dorset people as with most Eskimos the figures are usually naked.

There are several Dorset culture combs known to us, and some have human faces carved on them. These faces have distinctly Eskimo features, though there is a strong tendency to depict exaggeratedly flaring nostrils. This may, however, be a representation of some spirit being. We can say

9 **Man's knife handle.** Ivory (14 cm long). The blade was probably made of slate. From the Punuk Islands, Bering Sea, about A.D. 1000–1200. (The Museum of Primitive Art, New York)

10 **Ivory masquette** (9 × 3.5 × 2 cm). From the Tyara site, Sugluk, Quebec. Dorset culture. (National Museum of Man, Ottawa)

11 **Woman with a top-knot.** Walrus tooth (8.1 cm high). From the Thule district, Greenland. Probably Dorset culture, about 700 B.C.–A.D. 1300. (Danish National Museum, Copenhagen)

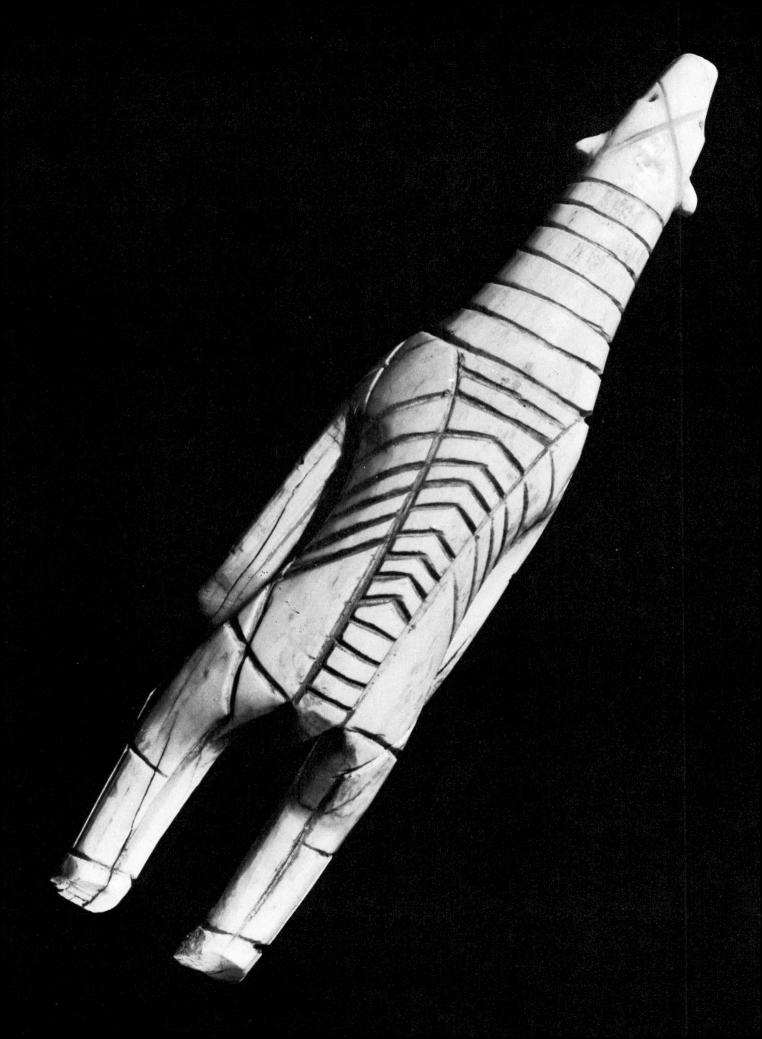

nothing about Dorset religion or language. There is
nothing of certainty. Several ivories show bear-man
figures, and some wooden masks have been found in
recent years. The wooden masks, usually quite well
carved, represent Eskimo facial types like the combs.
It seems as if some shamanistic religion was expressed
by these things; there even exist some ivory cases
which are of a type known to have been used by
Eskimo shamans in later times. (The shaman is a
particular kind of 'medicine man' found in primitive
societies who acts as magician, priest, doctor and
artist. He plays a vital role in the life of the community
who believe, for instance, that he can influence the
success of hunting expeditions or ward off illness by
communicating with the 'other world'.)

Of weapons, all the early cultures used harpoons,
though the Dorset people, with their penchant for
whale meat, made some of the finest harpoon heads,
foreshafts and butts. They used bow and arrows for
land hunting, and since they had no dogs it seems
that they must have been masters of the art of stalking
game. In some areas of northern Canada they have
left behind alignments of stone cairns which appear
to have been a means of frightening caribou herds
into a desired lane where they could be picked off by
the hunters. Possibly the women and children stood
behind some of the stone heaps shouting and waving
to scare the animals along the lanes. In some cases,
especially around the Boothia Peninsula, they were
aided by stone men, made of slabs of rock carefully
piled to represent human beings. It is also possible
that some of these stone giants were used as place
markers to guide people going to and from the hunting
grounds. They have no place in modern folklore and
no history, but stand like giants, at least by Eskimo
standards.

It may be that the people of the Dorset culture
were the inspiration for some recent Eskimo folk
tales about the Tornrit, a race of stupid people who
did not know how to make proper boots but wrapped
their legs in strips of skin. They are seen as a kind of
bogy-men. In Greenland, however, the Tornrit seem
to be identified with the Norse settlers of the eleventh
century.

The slow changes in the Dorset culture are not
properly understood because the sites where
excavation is practicable are few and far apart. There
is likely to be some sign of development in the earlier
period and decline in the later, not on theoretical
grounds, but for geographical reasons. The period
from 1000 B.C. to A.D. 1000 witnessed at first a steady
improvement in climate, and, towards the end, the
first symptoms of the approaching return to colder
conditions. This must have greatly influenced life for
these hunters of the frozen sea, at first by making the

13

12–13 Polar bear (back and front views). Typical skeletal motif, with the
bear shown swimming or possibly flying. Behind the sliding lid is
a secret compartment in the throat containing red ochre, probably
symbolising the blood of life. The legs have human characteristics
which suggest that this is a shaman in disguise. Walrus ivory
(3.2 × 15.7 × 3.6 cm). From the Alarnerk settlement, Igloolik area,
N.W.T. Dorset culture, about A.D. 500. (National Museum of Man,
Ottawa)

15

14 Stone men are found in northern Canada, particularly in the region of the Boothia Peninsula. Their purpose is not clear, but was probably connected with hunting the caribou. Probably Dorset culture.

15 Stone images by Kiakshuk. Artist's proof of stencil print. Cape Dorset, N.W.T., mid 20th century. (Gimpel Collection)

arctic more open to whales, and later by restricting their entry. There is no doubt that whale hunting was a mainstay of the Dorset period, though in the summer months when the inland areas of moss were free there was much organised caribou hunting. Something of that way of life survived among the peoples to the west of Hudson Bay until modern times. However, we must constantly remember that the Dorset people, without dogs, were likely to have lived in very small settlements because of the limitation on travel. The hunters had a comparatively limited area in which to gain a living for the people, and so there must have been a tendency to live in small villages without very much contact with strangers. The period when it was possible for larger groups to operate together was the summer when the whale hunts would make co-operation profitable, and the use of the skin boats, the umiaks, which could

17

carry ten or a dozen people, made contact by coastal travel feasible.

It seems likely that some of the Dorset people of the northern Canadian area developed the ice hut, the igloo, for winter shelter. It may have developed from snow blocks piled around skin tents. In the igloo, temperatures often rose to the heat of a European summer, though the atmosphere was smoky owing to the stone bowls in which blubber was kept burning through moss wicks. People went naked indoors, and the Dorset culture figurines only rarely show traces of clothing. There are some very few ivories showing ithyphallic males, but we could not describe the Dorset people as practising any erotic art. Like the historic Eskimos, they probably lived a natural sex life which needed no ceremonial stimulus.

The spread of the Dorset culture from the Bering Sea as far as Greenland covered a couple of centuries, but we should not think in terms of a determined drive to the east. The process was probably limited to the arrival of small groups of one or two families, who settled, hunted, and occasionally travelled. The short journeys did not imply a continuous periodic migration, but visits and return to home. The carrying of culture did not mean an advance by warlike bands imposing new ideas on the aboriginal people, but rather of visits and exchange of ideas. It is quite feasible that the spread of culture was simply a matter of the spread of new fashions which one village learned from another and passed on in turn to the other known neighbours. In historic times, a man who had travelled to many different settlements was known as a great traveller. It was usual to know of only two or three other groups of Eskimos; and it is probable that travel was equally limited in Dorset times.

The archaeologist has some difficulty in excavating the sites of Dorset culture. They are all coastal, and are all on slight rises in the ground where the vista allowed a look-out to be kept for game either on land or sea. All are in the region of permafrost which, although a great preservative, presents problems for the excavator. Only in the height of summer can a few inches of soil be removed, and then during the next afternoon the sun may soften another inch or so, and for an hour or perhaps two another tiny layer from an ancient midden is exposed. The work is controlled scientifically much more easily under these conditions, but it is painfully slow. At some sites there is steady erosion by the sea, and a dig is something in the nature of rescue archaeology. However, points of excavation are few, and it is abundantly clear that a great deal more has to be done before we can truly evaluate the standing of the Dorset culture of the arctic.

17

18

16 **Bear family** by Pauta. Green stone (18 × 14 × 11.5 cm). Cape Dorset, N.W.T., 1956–1957. (Collection: Mr and Mrs John K.B. Robertson, Ottawa)

17 **Ivory weasel**, probably used as a charm (1.7 × 5.7 × 1 cm). From Pingerluk, N.W.T.; **Pair of ivory swans**, probably gambling counters (1 × 6.1 × 2.3 cm). From Mansel Island, N.W.T. Both Dorset culture. (National Museum of Man, Ottawa)

18 **Ivory comb with face** (6.3 × 2.5 × 0.7 cm). From Maxwell Bay, N.W.T.; **Wooden spirit being** (11.7 × 1.7 × 0.9 cm). From Button Point site, Bylot Island, N.W.T. Both Dorset culture. (National Museum of Man, Ottawa)

The Northlanders

When Erik the Red quarrelled with his neighbours and would not abide by the laws of Iceland he was exiled. With several boatloads of friends and foreigners he set out for Greenland. Some were wrecked on the east coast, but Erik landed on the west coast. He found a fine country with a fiord containing green meadows enough to feed his cattle. There were no people around, no sign of the fur-clad natives, but on the beach he noted some stone arrowheads. Those arrowheads had been left by people of the Dorset culture who, with the return of a warm climatic spell, had moved northwards to continue their life hunting the creatures along the edges of the ice.

Archaeologists have found that just about this time, A.D. 1000, the people of northern Greenland, at Thule, underwent a change in their culture. Eskimos coming from the west had brought new things which their distant cousins in Alaska had discovered a couple of centuries earlier. The progress of the new ideas was still very slow because of the impossibility of moving quickly from one area to another except in summer, and possibly because of the hostility of the older population of Dorset culture people. The newcomers brought the dog, the dog-sledge, and the single-seater kayak. They relied more on seal and walrus for their food than on whale, though inland they still hunted mammals in summer, but with less emphasis on the caribou. However, the warm climate was coming to an end, and the caribou were not so frequent along the shores of the Arctic Ocean, and as they moved inland they came less within the range of the sea hunters. But the hardy musk ox was available throughout the area. The change in the balance of nature made it necessary to adapt a little, and it appears that the Dorset people had not changed their ways sufficiently, and eventually had to adopt the ideas of the bringers of the new Thule culture.

We do not know whether the people of the Thule and Dorset cultures were conscious of being one race. The difference between their ways of life was considerable. On the whole the modern Eskimo view is that their folk tales reflect the past rather well. If that is so, the newcomers viewed the older people as incompetent and uncivilised. Certainly there was a radical change in art styles. The deep grooves cut in surfaces no longer appear, the degree of stylisation is less, and the curved surfaces are more gentle. Moreover, the quantity of works of art seems to decrease. We gain the impression that these people, with the means of life extended by the use of sledge and dog, were facing a hard struggle with the climate and were so busy that few works of art were made in leisure time, now so scant that all effort was directed to the hunt.

As the climate became worse, the northern peoples of Baffin Island and Greenland found their way southward, and came into contact with the Norsemen in the regions around the southern fiords. Surviving legends tell of bitter conflict, of Eskimo resentment at barbarous raids by the strangers and of revenge killings. The cultural exchange seems to have been minimal. There were a few carvings made of people in strange clothes, including some with hats in fourteenth-century European fashion, but they are not numerous.

There was no chance of the two races ever understanding one another. The Europeans, suffering from the effects of the climatic failure, were clinging desperately to their own culture: church going, clothing of a Norse type, and plank-built boats. And they were still able to keep up a little contact through an annual trading vessel from Denmark. All in all they despised the little savages who lived like trolls. The Thule people had little to learn from the Norsemen. Perhaps some ideas about the construction of roofs in huts came to them. Their skin kayaks and umiaks were more adaptable than the wooden boats of the big men, and their paddles were more efficient than oars. Skin clothing was as good as anything the others had. In hunting the Eskimos were more efficient. And they were ready to repay the Norsemen for their cruelty. In the end there was fierce fighting, but the final victory was not glorious. The Norse settlers were undernourished, dwarfed and crippled with rickets. They could have made little resistance. As the last messengers from the Greenland settlements came to Rome, Christopher Columbus was setting out for the Indies. The northern sea

---

19 Drawing of an Eskimo by the Elizabethan voyager, John White.

20

21

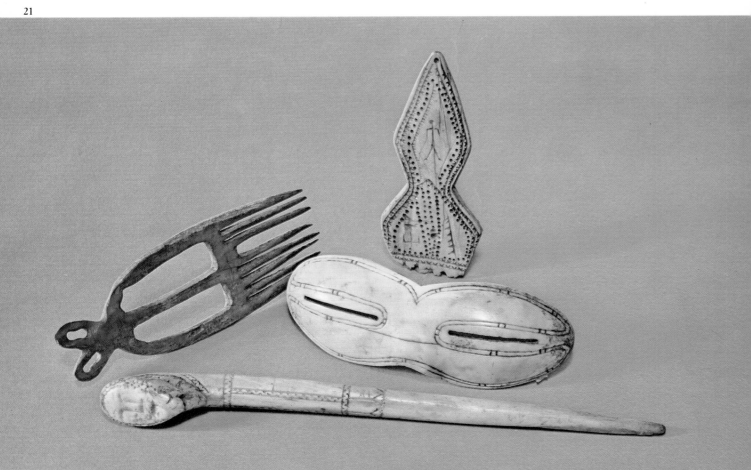

20 Hunters by Parr. Stone cut (61 × 91.5 cm). Cape Dorset, N.W.T., 1969.

21 Group of ivory objects : Marrow pick (1.9 × 20.4 × 2.7 cm). From south side of Strathcona Sound, N.W.T.; **Comb** (12 × 4.55 × 0.55 cm). From the Sleeper Islands, Hudson Bay; **Engraved comb bridge** (10.4 × 4.3 × 0.6 cm). From Igloolik, N.W.T.; **Snow goggles** (4 × 11.5 × 1.7 cm). From Maxwell Bay, N.W.T. All Thule culture. (National Museum of Man, Ottawa)

22 Aleut hunting hat of painted wood with incised ivory, beads and sea-lion whiskers. Not only did the cap shield the eyes from dazzle, it also afforded magic protection. From Alaska, about 1850. (Museum of the American Indian, New York)

23 Ivory two-man pendant (4.6 × 2.35 × 1.05 cm); **Ivory ornament,** possibly a wound plug (5.6 × 1.35 × 0.9 cm). From Maxwell Bay, N.W.T.; **Ivory ornament** (4.65 × 1.9 × 0.3 cm). From Belcher Islands, Hudson Bay. All Thule culture. (National Museum of Man, Ottawa)

22

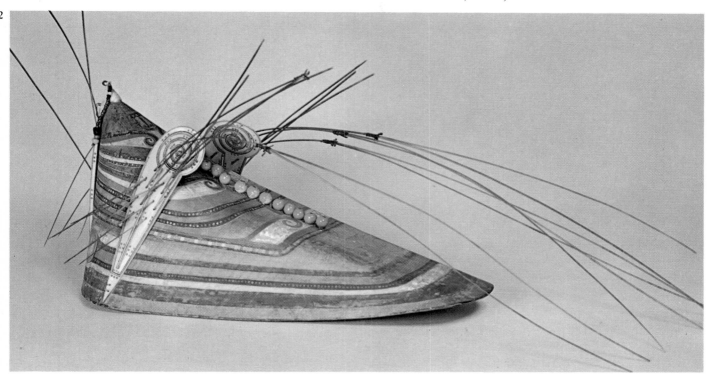

23

hunters were not to enjoy peace for long.

It was at about this period that the Eskimos achieved their most southern settlements when they established themselves in parts of northern Newfoundland and on the Labrador coast. These people, like the southern Alaskans, had access to growing trees, but they did not stay for very long in the new environment and moved north again among the barren rocks and icy hunting grounds they knew so well.

One of the serious effects of the falling in world temperatures in the thirteenth century was that whales in the arctic seas became rare. The open summer seas in which the great animals were hunted by large groups of people in umiaks were more and more restricted. The Thule people were forced to rely more on seal and walrus in the sea and caribou and fish inland. This meant that the grouping of families possible where whales were plentiful was no longer useful. The developed Thule culture is more and more found in small sites around a centre where the animals could be hunted successfully. If there were too many people the food supply for them would be insufficient, so two or three families would constitute a unit. Contacts with other people were rare, though inbreeding did not become much of a problem. The rare social visits were occasions of sexual courtesy which did much for the health of the families. However, the isolation of the small family units meant that everybody was fully occupied in obtaining a living and in making practical objects. They did not have any time for art for art's sake, but faced so many dangers and difficulties that they charmed many objects of everyday use by carving and incising on them heads of animals and pictures of successful hunts. There was a steady output of carved gambling counters, and a few charms were made to attract food animals, or to point out to the spirit world that the people needed help.

The problems of the polar north were reflected, no doubt, in other areas. But in Alaska the pattern of life was richer. The Pacific, which was open for longer periods, supplied whale, and hunting in the umiak was an important feature of life. The natives of the Alaskan mainland coasts varied a great deal among themselves, mostly for geographical and ecological reasons. They were all true Eskimos, though as usual they lived in widely separated groups. On the southern Alaskan coast they had fairly close contact with groups of Tlingit Indians, and adopted some cultural ideas, masks, and house types from them, although the relationships were hardly friendly. The country was well wooded, and the Eskimos built semi-subterranean family houses which served as permanent headquarters, though they used skin tents when away hunting in the summer. However, their main living came from the sea.

Northwards, towards the delta of the Yukon river, timber became more scarce, and the small Eskimo communities lived in any area where there was good access to the sea and where sea hunting was good. They also used fixed-home houses even if a village was only of five to ten households. These were often built of slabs of stone and masses of earth, with a window over the low tunnel-like entrance. The people lived mainly by sea hunting, but occasionally they ascended the rivers to hunt caribou and deer. However, in this inland region they felt ill at ease and were often involved in bloody conflict with bands of Kutchin Indian hunters. As far as possible they avoided contact and preferred to work from their own coastal areas. Such a way of life was hardly comparable with that of the other Eskimo regions. This cultural disparity is clear throughout the archaeological record. At every stage, the house ruins of western Alaska were larger and better appointed than those of other communities.

Around the rocky north west coast of Alaska to the low clay soils and mudflats of Point Barrow there were ice hunters who conformed more to the usual pattern of Eskimo life. In the Bering Strait area there were Eskimo hunting communities settled on the island of St. Lawrence, and on the Diomede Islands. They were all sea hunters who spent the shorter winter seasons in ice hunting over the frozen sea. From early times there was an ancient trade route across the Bering Strait between peoples from Siberia and Indians from southern and central Alaska.

In the Bering Sea area the Aleut people were a special group of arctic fisher folk. They spoke a language grammatically close to the Inuit of the Eskimo, but with a very different vocabulary. Their homes on the Aleutian Islands and the western tip of the Alaska peninsula determined their close relationship to the sea. They were the most southerly relatives of the Eskimos, living in a region far below the Arctic Circle, where the Pacific Ocean is rarely frozen. They developed larger and more efficient skin boats, including a multiple-seater kayak, wore fine waterproof skin clothing for fishing expeditions and utilised timber and bark. Their art was very individual, but many motifs seemed to echo the swirling curves of the Old Bering Sea culture, though it is unlikely that there was any direct contact across such a great expanse of time. One of their more famous art products was the bark eye-shade, a pyramidal hat of birch bark adorned with painted patterns and seal whiskers.

Although, in a sense, each Eskimo group had an individual culture, in the early historical period they

24 Carved wooden death mask. From Unalaska Island. Aleut, before 1869. (Smithsonian Institution, Museum of Natural History, Washington D.C.)

25

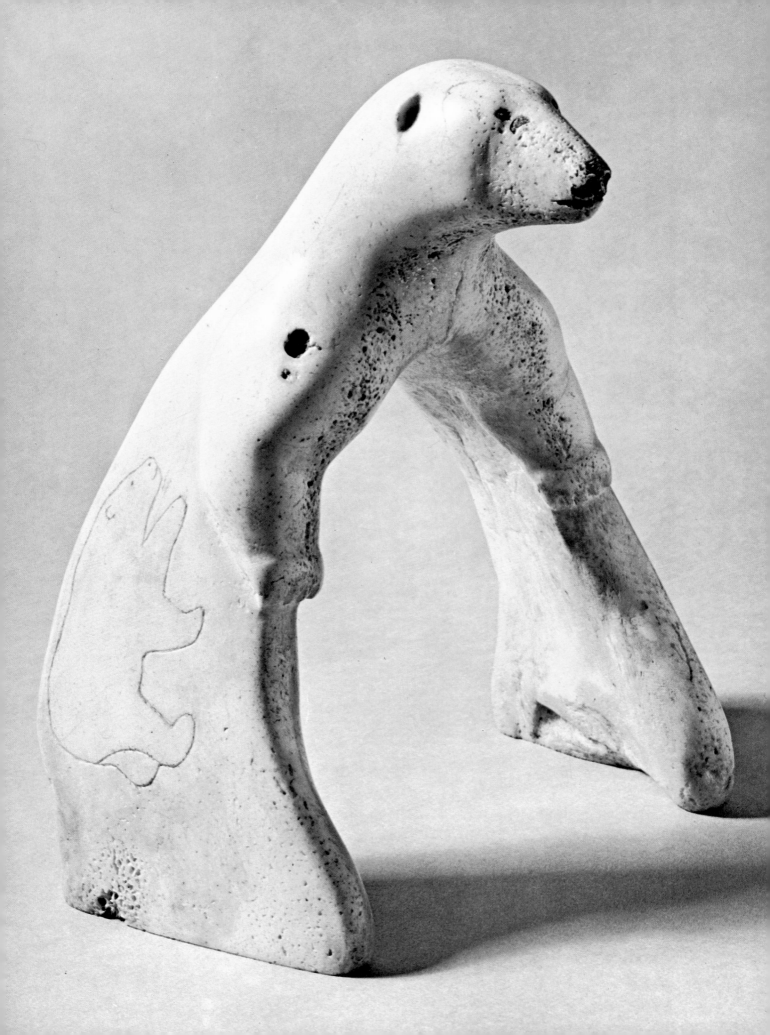

25 **Polar bear.** Whale skeleton. From the Canadian arctic, mid 20th century. (Gimpel Collection)
26 **Inua mask** representing the spirit of a salmon. Worn as part of a shamanistic ceremony to bring success in salmon fishing. Painted wood and feathers (48 cm high). From Alaska, probably 19th century. (André Breton Collection, Paris)

26

27

had a common basis in the Thule culture. There were, however, two unusual variants which are of importance. At the mouth of the Coppermine River in north western Canada the Eskimos produced tools of copper. They were a rare example of people using metal with a Stone Age technique. As far as the Eskimos were concerned the green-stained nodules of natural copper were stones, but with the special property of malleability. It was possible to hack at one of the copper boulders until a piece could be wrenched off, and the soft stone did not break when hammered, but spread out as if it were some kind of paste. With hammering, smoothing with stones and filing on coarser stones, the copper made very adequate harpoon points, knives and fishhooks. The metal was a convenient material for use, but was not so remarkable that it was used in any other region. The few visitors who came do not seem to have returned for trade. An Eskimo aesthetic based on practical shapes for use determined that the copper implements had similar forms to those made from slate. Indeed, in actual practice copper was no more useful than slate. Neither did the metal have much use in producing works of art except that a few ivory figurines were fitted with copper studs in lips and cheeks where the local women would have worn stone ones. It was the malleability and toughness which made the local copper an attractive material. No one has any record of the poisonous qualities of its oxides. The metal was never heat treated because the Eskimos had no means of creating a high temperature. The flame from the usual blubber lamp was hot enough to boil water but nothing much more. In the few places in Alaska where a coarse pottery was made, wood fires were available, but among the Copper Eskimos, burning wood would have been a wasteful use of material brought by the sea for use in making tools and weapons.

The other aberrant group were the very old-fashioned Caribou Eskimos who lived in the barren lands north west of Hudson Bay. They had apparently deliberately decided to reduce dependence

28

on seal hunting and concentrated on following the caribou herds as they passed on their way to summer or winter pastures. There was land hunting in which the animals were driven by all the free members of the group towards the hunters. As in Dorset times, piles of stones were erected which the animals mistook for hunters. These served to channel the path of the animals in the right direction. However, the hunts were never exterminating attacks; always sufficient animals were left to escape to keep the food supplies ready for later years. At river crossings much used by the caribou, the Eskimos hunted them with spear thrower and lance propelled from a kayak. On occasion the Caribou Eskimos made snow huts, but usually they lived in their skin tents, reinforced by snow blocks in winter. They were constantly busy with their hunting life, but produced a number of small carvings both useful and magical. In some ways they were akin to the Dorset culture, but in all important aspects they were Thule culture people with the dog-sledge and kayak as their means of

transport. Their very small bands of a few families of caribou hunters must have resembled in many ways the tundra hunters of the last Ice Age in Europe.

The most remarkable group of all were the inhabitants of north west Greenland. They were typical people of the Thule culture, and had adapted to the heavy ice of the far north as well as the grim darkness of the months of winter night. It appears that they had been part of a general eastward movement of Eskimo groups, and it may well be that they also included some southern Greenlanders who had moved northwards in the period of optimum climate in late Dorset times. They were discovered by Eskimos from the Pond Inlet region of Baffin Island as late as the 1860s. By this time, whalers were operating in the arctic seas and the Pond Inlet people

27 **Kneeling caribou** by Piluardjuk. Ivory (12 × 14 × 2.5 cm). Repulse Bay, N.W.T., 1960–1962. (Collection: Mr and Mrs D. F. Wright, Ottawa)
28 **Kayaks and caribou** by Angosaglo and Ikseegah. Print. Baker Lake, N.W.T., 1972.

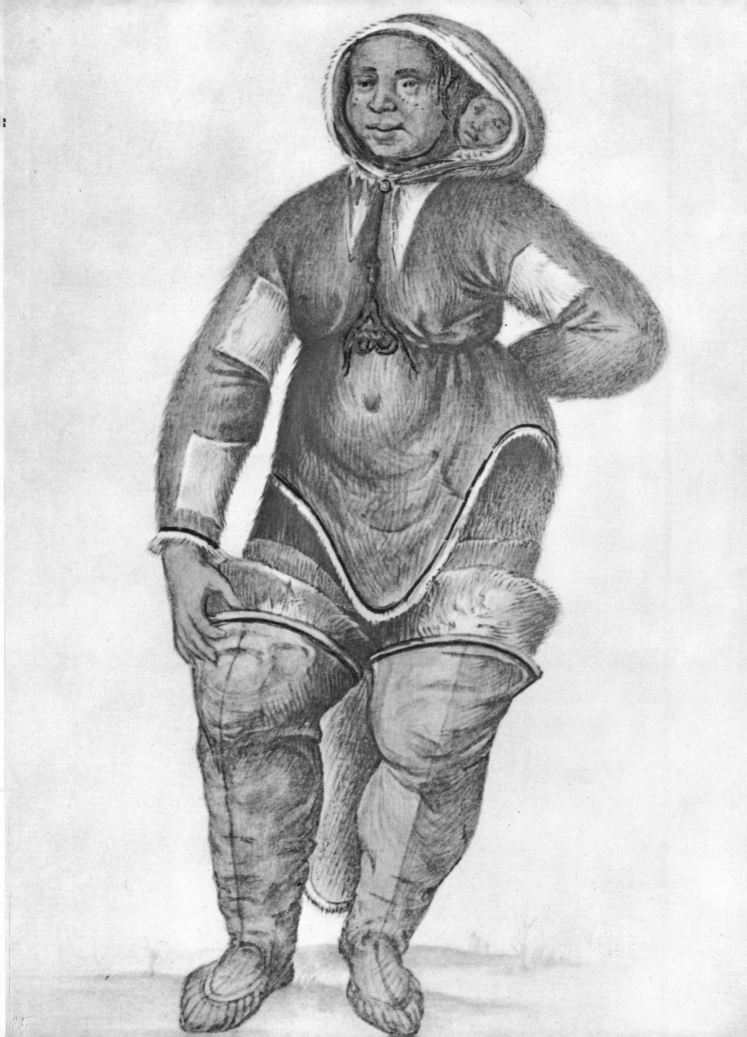

29 Eskimo woman in furs with a baby on her back. Watercolour by the Elizabethan voyager, John White. Note the facial tattoo and three layers of leg covering.

30 Eskimo recollection. Ochre and grey stone (2 × 12 × 12 cm). Port Harrison, Quebec, 1951. (Collection: Ian Graham Lindsay, Ottawa)

31 Whale-bear-bird monster. Green stone. From the Canadian arctic, mid 20th century. (Gimpel Collection)

30

31

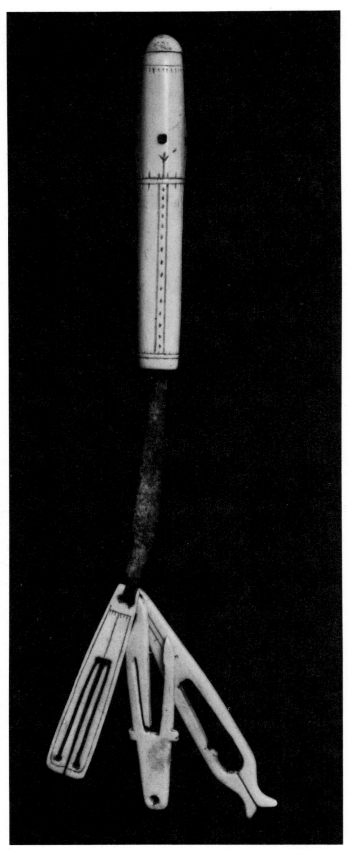

heard from them of other Eskimos far away in the north. They determined to visit them, and made the long journey from the Canadian arctic across Devon Island and Ellesmere Island to Smith Sound. In just such a way their ancestors may have occasionally moved, either to find better hunting grounds or to meet other human beings in the great loneliness of the ice. This journey of over seven hundred miles was achieved by a compact group of a few families who simply travelled until they achieved their objective. Hunting was good all the way and they knew the general direction in which to go, through the stories of the whalers.

On reaching the Polar Eskimos of Smith Sound, they found them backward indeed. To the Polar people, the Pond Inlet Eskimos must have seemed wonderful, for they brought long forgotten arts with them. It seems almost incredible that the Polar people had no knowledge of the multi-pronged leister for fishing, nor of the kayak, nor of hunting caribou with bow and arrow, nor how to hunt on the open sea when the ice melted. Archaeologists have shown that long ago their ancestors could build kayaks, but apparently under polar conditions the short period of open water made the labour of kayak building not worthwhile. In any case, during the climatic regression of the thirteenth century it is possible that the ice never melted at all in north Greenland.

It is quite clear from archaeology that there had been many movements of Eskimo groups around Greenland, and no simple theory of migration can account for the distribution of culture sites. However, this last cultural migration and influence of culture contact is recorded and gives a good example of the kind of travel which had occasionally occurred throughout history.

At the eastern end of the continent the people of Greenland had not only moved southwards, but also took cultural ideas westwards and modified the cultures of the people around Hudson Bay. But we must remember that although designs appear to have been spread in planned movements, the fact is that actual contacts must have been rare and that there was a good deal of local development in which practical needs determined similar alterations of design in tools and weapons. For instance, the whole central area was much more devoted to caribou hunting and fishing than other areas, and the people were forced into seasonal migrations. Whereas the Eskimos on the edge of the open sea were more settled, and their culture was centred more on the whale and the walrus. And some of the West Coast Eskimos were so close to the groups of American Indians that they almost merged.

32 Ivory needlecase. Western Eskimo, 19th century. (Museum of Mankind, London)

33 Wooden mask representing Negakfok the cold weather spirit, the Eskimo equivalent of Jack Frost. (92 cm high). From the Kuskokwim river area, Alaska. (Museum of the American Indian, New York)

During the whole period of prehistory, the artists of the northlands had been a people of the Mesolithic hunting culture. Their finest work was the result of infinite patience, using stone tools and sometimes burnishers of polished stone. They devised many forms of scrapers and knives, and in particular a long side-bladed knife which was laid along the whole forearm so that an even pressure could be applied. They not only carved in soft driftwood and bone, but also made wonderful things from ivory. The ivory tusk of the narwhal, the great tusks of the walrus and teeth from the seal all formed marvellous material for the artist, who was probably a shaman as well. Most of the carvings were quite small, and their shapes were usually little altered from the original form of the ivory used. The shape of a tooth was easily turned into an animal head. Bones made longer figures, such as were needed when making arrow-

34-35 **Small ivory charms** in the shape of a polar bear and a seal, probably sympathetic magic for hunting. Probably from the Canadian arctic, 19th century. (James Hooper Collection)
36 **Ivory drum handle.** (14 cm long). Probably from the north coast of Alaska. (Museum of Mankind, London)
37 **Drum dancer** by Bernadette Iguptaq. Grey stone and bone (9.5 × 5 × 13.5 cm). Repulse Bay, N.W.T., 1963–1964. (The Twomey Collection, Government of Manitoba)

straighteners. Hard stone was sometimes polished into shape, but the form used was normally a pendant which could be used for flaking the edges of tools of flint. Soft stone was carved to make the saucers and dishes which were used as lamps and cooking stoves. Small figures of wood and ivory, and only very rarely of stone, are known, but they are comparatively infrequent. From northern Alaska some masks made of pieces of bone, carved and fitted into a wooden frame, have been found. Masks were usually tiny amulets, but full-sized wooden masks are known and also some made of the cancellar tissue of whale limb bones and skulls. These, however, derive mainly from Alaska.

All in all, if we were to consider the archaeological records without any further evidence we should be forced to think of the ice hunters of the Dorset and Thule cultures as people showing a development through time, mostly involved in making practical tools and useful artefacts, but from time to time producing objects of high artistic quality. They would be seen as a practical race of ice hunters, who had artistic ability but little time to develop their art. The mainspring of their art we would guess to be the cult of spirits concerned with success in the food quest; but the legends and folklore behind their way of life, and the living force inspiring the artists would remain unknown.

At the height of the Thule culture the Eskimos were self sufficient. They had no need of outside contact, though metal was a desirable novelty. On the whole they preferred to be apart from other humans, and most of them were so isolated that they were to all appearances the only people in the universe. Their art remained very practical, but they devoted a part of their time to making representations of people, animals and the beings of their spirit world. Every work of art had life and a spiritual meaning, and every individual might be an artist.

The groups of people living by hunting must not be so big that the game was insufficient. If a settlement grew big some people hived off to find new hunting areas. If the game failed, people strove to keep alive. But often whole settlements died quietly in the snow; they joined the spirit world which was so near. In that land of chasing mists and blue skies, of sun and stars, of strange noises on the ice and the ever dancing aurora, the inner personality of the people was unusually free to experience dreams and visions. The more sensitive people became shamans (the Eskimo word is angakoq) who would prophecy while in trance, self-induced by drumming on the big seal-membrane drums. Other people would discover that they were helped by protective spirits and would call on them in any trouble.

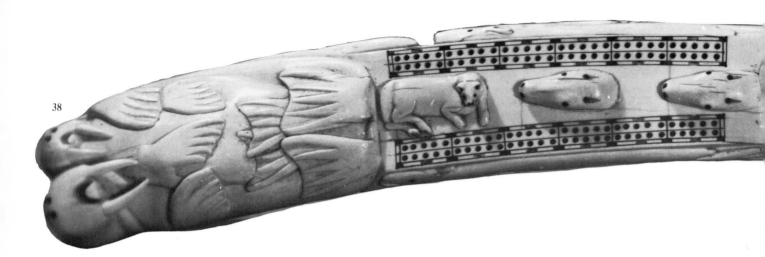

38 Ivory cribbage board decorated with sea creatures said to have originated from the fingers of Sedna, the great mother under the sea. From Alaska, 19th century. (Cincinnati Art Museum. Gift of Samuel Ach)

Eskimo religion was a complex of beliefs which were accepted all over the arctic. Each group might have some individual beliefs, but as a whole the people had similar ideas about the supernatural world which was always so close to them. There were no fixed ceremonials, no sacred days, but many hearts rejoiced when the sun reappeared after the long arctic winter night. On the days before migration to summer or winter hunting areas there were dances and, of course, much questioning of the spirits about the nature of the coming season. Under the sea was a great mother figure, usually called Sedna, whose fingers and toes became the sea creatures. She was always creating life, and was always aware of what happened to her creatures. The animals were not just things to be destroyed and eaten, but living beings who showed intelligence. Their souls were important and had to be placated. A captured seal was addressed thankfully that it had given its life for the people, and a piece of skin was specially cut and left behind as a symbol of the hope for a renewal of living seals. Birds, caribou, musk oxen, foxes, hares, freshwater char, and great whales were all part of the living world. The hunter by observation achieved a certain degree of identification with his quarry, and this is reflected in the art he produced to bring them to his net. He himself was part of this living world and so he never violated it, never killed for pleasure, and never took life without thought and prayer for new life. So near to the basic subsistence of the wild he had a respect for all living things: hence a certain gentleness of character which he displayed in his everyday living.

It is the belief in the unity of all living things

which gives so strong a human appeal to Eskimo art. The images are not simply forms or representations; they are not the sole product of the conscious fraction of human personality, but the expression of an inner world which the Eskimo has experienced through the ages. The shaman is believed to be able to visit the land of souls, to find the great Mother under the sea, and to discuss with the spirits of seals, walruses and whales the ways of life. It is the universality of the ideas within Eskimo art which makes it acceptable to folk of other cultures. We find similar themes about man and nature preserved in ancient fairy tales and legends which were once stories of the gods. We remember that the Northern gods were once shape changers and knew the thoughts of the birds and beasts.

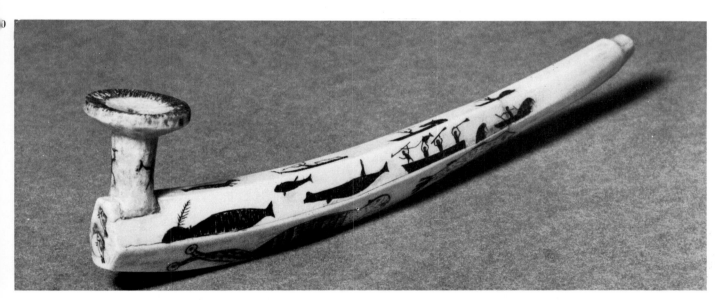

The first work of Eskimo art known to have been treasured in Europe came from an excavation of a house destroyed by the fire of 1413 in Bergen. The little ivory walrus came from a layer well below the fire zone and is thought to have belonged to the twelfth or thirteenth century. Brought by a Norseman from the land of the Skraelings, it was once a link between hunter and hunted in an Eskimo tent.

The last phase of the Thule culture was to be observed by strangers from other lands, by men who scratched pictures on whales' teeth as a leisure activity, and who often enough died in the arctic because they could not live like the people whom they called Eskimos. Their evidence is to be found in many books of travel and exploration. Among them were artists who depicted the strange world of ice

and snow where people clad in furs lived in skin tents and marvellous domed houses of snow blocks. From the beginning of contact the Eskimos became famous, and romantic images of them filled the European mind.

It is quite obvious to us now that those Eskimos of the travellers' tales were the people of the Thule culture and the ancestors of the Eskimos of today. Nothing in the archaeological record shows any major difference. The physical remains of the people are indistinguishable, though we must remember that all the peoples of the north are physically much the same through all the changes of culture. What the modern Eskimos adopted from the previous Thule people is not certain. It may be that the snow-built igloo of the Canadian arctic is a development of a

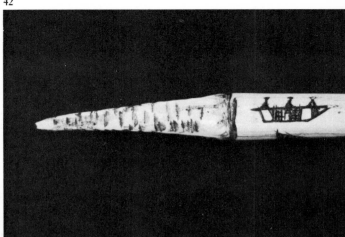

Thule construction. Certainly the use of the umiak type of boat persisted, together with snow goggles, snow knives and harpoon types, though the decoration on them is in a new style. But all these articles are necessary to life by the arctic seas.

With the arrival of the explorers, archaeology suddenly turned into history. It was an interesting time because the arctic was changing once more. The worst of the cold period, which had destroyed the Greenland settlements around Eiriksfiord, was slowly receding. The summer ice covered less and less sea each year. In the sixteenth century, Frobisher went to the arctic and reached Ungava Bay, then the limit of navigation, though now it is by no means the end of open sea, not for a thousand miles. Frobisher had some unpleasant experiences with the Eskimos, who tended to ambush the visitors and shoot bone-pointed arrows into them. No doubt they thought these sailors were a party of returning Norsemen whom they looked upon as bloodthirsty barbarians. Yet there was peace at times long enough for the artist John White to make records of Eskimos as persons as well as an attacking party threatening a boat's crew.

Everything about the Eskimos depicted by John White shows them to have been indistinguishable from modern Eskimos – or at least from their grandparents. The costumes were similar, the weapons just the same. Similarly the elegant little skin kayaks were noted and drawn. These Eskimos were not land lubbers, but quickwitted and active hunters who knew their country by sea even better than by land. They had skin tents, and wintered in snow-domed igloos. People wore tattoos, especially women, and their indoor dress was scanty. They were a well-greased people who smelt strongly of smoked fish, yet they were attractive to the visitors because of their personal qualities. There might have been fighting, but there was also trading and laughter. Importantly we note that under the terrible conditions

41

41 **Wooden ladle** showing a man shot through the middle and a spirit with evil intentions above. From Alaska, about 1890. (Museum of Mankind, London)
42 **Barbed spear point**, engraved with sea hunters in umiaks. Ivory. From the Canadian arctic. Acquired in 1933. (Horniman Museum, London)
43 **Europeans as seen by the Eskimos.** Wood (tallest 10 cm high). Found at Upernavik and Angmagssalik, Greenland. 14th–19th century. (Danish National Museum, Copenhagen)

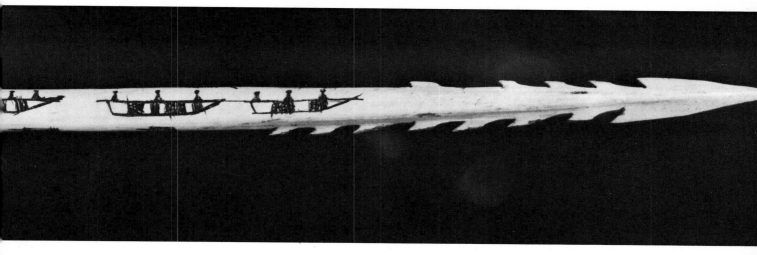

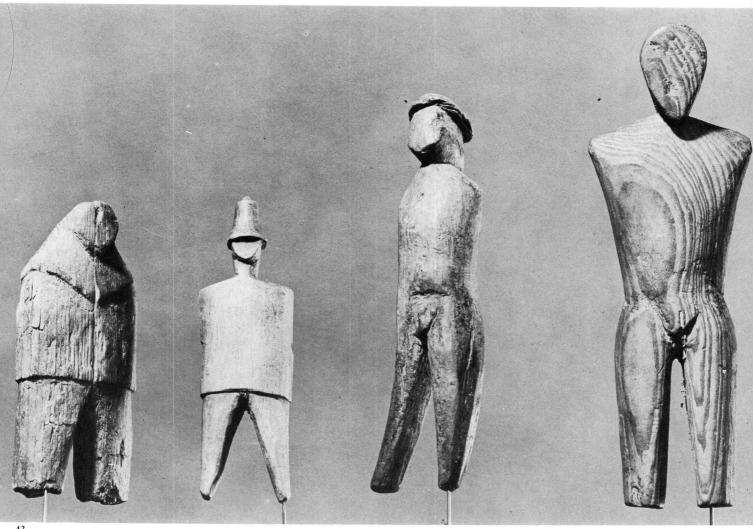

43

of the arctic coasts the white men had little advantage
over the Eskimos, and so it was possible for the two
groups to respect each other. Neither were the
numbers of people involved ever very large. Under
the optimum conditions where Eskimo communities
were able to unite in whale hunts there were rarely as
many as two hundred people involved. Usually the
isolated little groups of twenty or thirty people

presented but a small threat to any ship's crew
sojourning among them. Neither did most sailors
present any threat to the Eskimos. Sometimes
goods were stolen, but more often there was trade
for metal nails, and strange foods in return for furs.
Most families welcomed sailors as temporary sexual
companions, and since they did not understand the
coarse humour of the seventeenth-century Europeans

they were not offended. It had been customary for uncountable ages to offer sexual consolation to visiting strangers. It was a two-way exchange of happiness of great value in the lonely and emotionally depressive conditions of the arctic nights. It was all so natural that Eskimo art has only a very mild erotic aspect. Neither can it be said that the seventeenth- and eighteenth-century Europeans were any cleaner than the smelly wild Eskimos. Such contacts between exploring expeditions from Europe and the Eskimos were rare and not the occasion of much cultural exchange. Some Eskimo ivory carvings found their way to cabinets of curiosities; some European knives came into service among the Eskimos.

The first explorers of the Eskimo lands were seeking gold. Martin Frobisher brought back a load of black earth which was thought to contain gold. It had been accepted by many intellectuals of those days that the *materia prima* from which gold could be extracted would be earthy and black. It was one of the basic assumptions of alchemy. Expectations were aroused, so there was little difficulty in equipping a larger expedition to Labrador to bring back more of the mineral. Alas, the assayers found so little gold that refining was not worth while. Yet the search went forward, on a strictly commercial basis, hoping for the enormous expected profits from a pirate-free north west passage to Cathay. In search of the vision of clear water, travellers faced the icy terrors, discovered Ungava and Baffin Island and the great

44

bay where Hendrik Hudson died with his son, abandoned in a small boat.

To those early explorers, the Eskimos were only incidental events, strange people who lived marvellously in the ice. They were thought of as cunning fighters who were bold and bloodthirsty. The sailors knew nothing of the tragic history of the old Viking settlements, but the echoes of those times lived among the Eskimos. French fishermen also contacted the Eskimos in the east, and there was the same mixture of trading for furs and fighting. Each side had possessions which were worth stealing if the opportunity offered. However, at the dawn of the seventeenth century it seemed that the white man would not try to pass the ice barriers of the northern

seas. The same barriers were the homeland of the Eskimos, the hunter's land of happiness and survival.

In the far west the story was similar; Japanese and Russian fishermen saw the Aleuts, and occasionally penetrated beyond to the more truly Eskimo settlements. But there could be no true meeting of minds and the total result of such contacts were a few folk tales, and the possession of some iron knife blades which the Eskimos had obtained through barter.

The first period of European contact with the Eskimos had little effect upon their lives. The ancient ways continued. The trading posts set up by the Hudson's Bay Company were of some importance as points where hunters could exchange skins for knives, but their contact with the Eskimos was much less than with the Indians of the southern areas beyond the Bay. Trade followed the forests and lakes where there were more valuable skins for barter. As for ivory and sealskins, the whalers were soon supplying the markets of Europe without any great necessity to trade with the small groups of Eskimos they met on their wanderings. The important contacts in those days were peripheral, some in Alaska, but mainly on the Atlantic seaboard of Labrador and Greenland.

The most important single event in this area was the missionary work of Hans Egede who worked in Greenland from 1721 to 1736. He began Eskimo education, and opened up the world of the white man in a friendly way. A little later, the Moravian Brethren came to Labrador. The missions with their good intentions and hard words produced only local effects. Some Christian symbols carved in ivory were made, but they did not appear outside the shores of the opening of the Davis Strait. Like all other Eskimo communities, the people were isolated by great distances one from another. The missions were foci of trade and became organised villages where people could find a living. But there was no incentive to seek out other Eskimos, no normal contact. As had been the case for thousands of years, this widely separated people retained much of the basic arctic culture, but developed as individual communities. However, by the mid 1860s Eskimo life was gradually changing through contact with the white men, the kabloona as they called them. Animals were being hunted for commercial reasons, and the ideas of the foreigners brought new influences on art and life. Only very remote people escaped it. The end of the Thule culture was approaching and a new way of Eskimo life was imminent.

44 **Singing psalms** by John Polik. Bone (6.3 × 10.8 × 6.3 cm). Eskimo Point, N.W.T., 1966. (Collection: Mr and Mrs D. F. Wright, Ottawa)

The Changing Arctic

The nineteenth century was a period of total change for the people of the northlands. The climate was becoming slightly warmer, and sea hunting became easier, but also the improved conditions revived the European search for a north west passage to Asia. The economics of Europe were changing and the greatly intensified search for trade included an increase in the fur trade. Most importantly of all, the United States of America was now a nation with an expanding population and all the needs of a civilised state comparable to the Canadian Dominion of Queen Victoria.

The Canadian arctic was the scene of many British exploring expeditions organised through the Admiralty. No doubt some strategic considerations influenced the mapping of the arctic, but in fact much of the work done showed the devotion of the leaders to pure science. The reports of the Parry Expedition, so well illustrated by drawings of people as well as maps, have given us a marvellous understanding of Eskimo life of the 1820s. The exploring expeditions were also of some interest to the Eskimos. They introduced new ideas, and gave an opportunity for trade, and for acquiring guns which helped the hunters. That hunting was likely to become destructively successful was not envisaged by either side. The Eskimos were still hunting only enough for their needs, but little by little those needs extended to the acquisition of skins for trade with the Europeans.

There was a certain equality between Eskimos and strangers, since, although the visitors possessed marvellous things, they were unable to support themselves in the arctic if they lost their ships. The melancholy fate of Sir John Franklin and all his expedition was watched by Eskimos over the few years which it took for all to die. Some of them were helped by groups of Eskimo hunters, but they moved on trying to reach some distant port where they would be rescued. But there was no success, and in later years the local people took other sailors to the graves of those kabloona whom they had buried. Such a tragedy made it quite clear that only the Eskimos could be safe in their world of ice.

However, the explorers were soon succeeded by ships of whale hunters. The growth of the civilised world whence these strange men came was now impinging on the arctic. Whalebone for corsets, seal-skins for coats and muffs and ivory for ornaments were all sought after and became the source of much good to the Eskimos who often worked for reward on ships and brought furs for exchange. Alas, too often they made the exchange for whisky and put themselves out of action while indulging their passion for the strange vision-bringing liquid. But their great tragedy came when the whalers responded to the call for more oil for lighting and for foodstuffs. At the turn of the century a cheaper substitute for butter was needed in Europe. The population increased during the Industrial Revolution in numbers but not in riches. A great deal of research went into turning whale oil into the new margarine. The result was not starvation for the Eskimos but an increasing market. And that in turn meant the establishment of larger groupings of villages at suitable places both for hunting and trading with the people from the big ships. Once more the wide spread of the arctic meant that many groups of Eskimos were not in contact with the strangers, but little by little new trade products, needles, metal tools, stoves and so on, became current utilities in the arctic.

This increase of contact in the Arctic Ocean was partly due to climatic improvement, and this had continued in Greenland until, by the mid nineteenth century, conditions were almost as they had been in the times of the Norse settlement at Brattahlid. Greenland was politically part of Denmark and trade with Danish ships was steady. The difference was largely that the Danes were first to try to assimilate Eskimo culture into European ways. Small towns grew up as centres. Missionary schools were followed by state schools. By the middle of the nineteenth century a newspaper was published in Upernavik using the Eskimo language. A local artist made a series of woodcuts to illustrate a little book about the end of the Norse settlements in Greenland. The population of southern and eastern Greenland was small but it had achieved a new northern way of life

45 Aleut baskets. The Aleut tradition of weaving small baskets and cases was stimulated by the demand during the 19th-century gold rushes. But it is now a dying art and examples are much sought after by collectors. These four baskets, covering bottles, are woven of grass with embroidery thread for the patterns. The tallest is 20 cm high. From the Aleutian Islands, early 20th century. (University of Alaska Museum, College, Alaska)

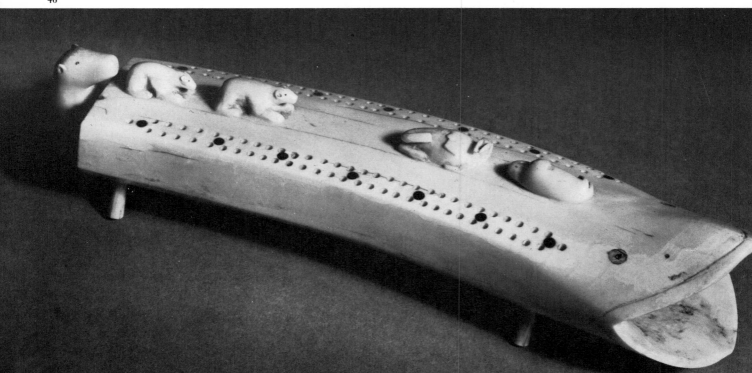

47

which was completely viable in the new world situation. Hunting and fishing were the mainstays of the commerce of Greenland, but at the same time Eskimo people were visiting Denmark and discovering much about the European at home. The artists were finding a market for occasional ivory trinkets and beautiful household ornaments. There were no great quantities of such works, but they were available and much enjoyed. Part of the change came from the fact that the Greenlanders were now Christian church members, and the old magical spur to art production was largely discounted. Hence there was no reticence in displaying abilities. Also there had been a general adaptation of costume in which European woollen garments were joined with the ancient skills in leatherwork to produce something typically Eskimo, yet of the newly developing world. In the late nineteenth century, Europeans found the Greenland belles quite exciting, displaying well rounded thighs dressed in delicate leather tracery at

the top of long boots. In their homeland the Europeans were still deeply stirred at the sight of a lady's ankles. But the Greenlanders did not bother; they had managed to adapt the utility of Eskimo clothing with elegance and beauty in their own way. In Greenland a composite culture was growing of which all the main elements were Eskimo. Yet such was the difficulty of the terrain and the vastnesss of the silent ice that no one was then aware of the Polar Eskimos still living their ancient hunting life at the other end of the great island. The material basis for a rapid development of the whole Eskimo population scattered around Greenland was not yet ready. However, in the south, around Angmagssalik in the east, and at Upernavik in the west, art was flourishing in a new context in Eskimo life.

The Siberian Eskimos, though few in number, had learned much from settlers from Asia who had brought designs of Russian folk art with them which suited their taste. They were also in contact

46 **Ivory knife handle** engraved with Europeans descending from a sailing ship. Probably from the Canadian arctic, mid 19th century. (City of Liverpool Museums)

47 **Cribbage board** carved from solid ivory with polar bears stalking a walrus asleep on the ice. Siberian Eskimo, late 19th century. (Collection: Hudson's Bay Company)

48 **Whip.** Siberian Eskimo, 19th century. (Museum of Mankind, London)

49 **Shaft straightener** with a handle in the shape of a bear's head. Ivory (16.5 cm long). From Alaska, mid 19th century. (Museum of Mankind, London)

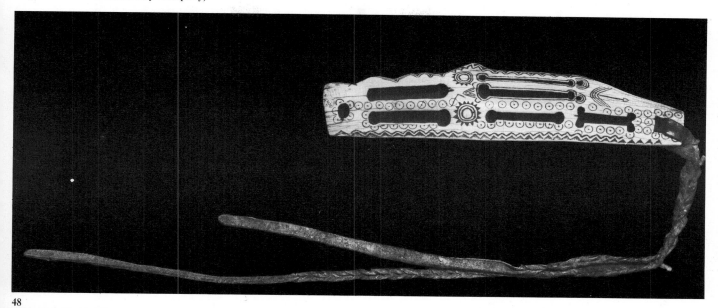

48

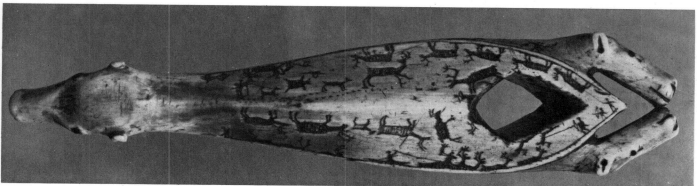

49

with the Chukchi and traded with them for tobacco pipes and for carving. In this area they had a rather unusual supply of carving material in the mammoth tusks which were sometimes exposed when the spring floods washed down clay and gravel banks. It would seem that the Siberian Eskimos, although few and isolated, were probably a westwards travelling group in ancient times from the American side of the Bering Strait. In historic times they had been in close contact with the whaling fleets in the Pacific, and developed the scrimshaw work they had learned from the sailors to a high degree of illustrative realism. In part this was an art for exchange with the sailors, but it also illustrated the themes of the stories and songs which were sung in the community houses during the winter. The elegance and beauty of their work made it very acceptable to the sailor and the diplomat. These Eskimos had a long contact with traders, and they had become fur trappers as well as hunters and fishermen for their standard subsistence.

The Eskimos of the west coast of North America also saw great changes during the nineteenth century. The Aleuts of the Bering Sea area had been in contact with other peoples for centuries: Japanese fishermen, exploring navigators including James Cook and the great Admiral Behring after whom the Strait was named, and Kotzebue whose interest in native artefacts resulted in a fine collection now in the Hermitage Museum in Leningrad.

The explorers had been followed up by the Russian government and the Orthodox Church, but the desolate lands of Alaska seemed of no great importance, and in 1857 Alaska was sold to the United States of America. By this time there were many ships from the United States and Canada cruising after whales, and it was in this sector of the Eskimo lands that the local people learned the art of scrimshaw decoration by engraving the surface of ivory and rubbing lamp-black into the lines. Some of their Thule culture ancestors had sometimes engraved

little pin-men figures in a very formal way, but this new art inspired by the spare-time art of the sailors encouraged individual self-expression. A new quality of scenic representation was achieved, and seal-ribs used as bows for bow drills became picture galleries of Eskimo life. Eskimo scrimshaw work does not necessarily reflect anything of European culture or religion. Most compositions are accounts of Eskimo living, and some show records of shamanistic magic. The spirits and non-material creatures take form but they are the same beings described in the ancient folk tales of the Eskimo. Naturally the Christian converts made some kind of religious art, simple and sincere works, often pendants and ornaments for Christian use.

Not all contacts between Eskimos and whalers were sweetness and light. There were raids and murder on wrecked ships, stealing of canvas to replace sealskin for the summer tents, and a new development of begging from the richer strangers. But the saddest blow to the Eskimos was the introduction of cheap whisky which became, as so often with people new to intoxicants, a dangerous curse. The desire for it induced cheating on both sides, and the effect was often dangerous, as when a group of islanders of the Bering Strait once went on a drunken feast and failed to bring in the autumn seal meat, so that in the following winter many died from starvation. Nevertheless the American Government was not unmindful of its protégés in the far north

west. Some attempts were made to help the local people to set up trading stations, and little by little schools were established.

The nineteenth century was one of change. In its course sailors and scientists added immensely to the world's store of knowledge about the Eskimo people. The great museums of the world have fine carvings and objects of everyday life from all the regions of the arctic. Some of them belong to the world of culture-contact and reflect the desire of the Eskimos to adopt something of Western living styles. There are also works which were made for exchange, some to amuse the sailors and others to go to the homes of white people who began to feel the charm of Eskimo art. They were good work, and honestly made, but they were falling between two ideals. They were neither the old magical art which assisted the hunter nor the highly paid art which expresses something of the inner personality of the artist. The level reached was simply of representation.

It is the everyday objects which were decorated with pictorial history and mythology that tell us most about Eskimo life in the nineteenth century before Eskimo culture was greatly changed. They show us that the shaman was still an important member of society who was at once here and also in the world of the spirits. His position was socially important, and it often brought wealth in the shape of presents of food and garments as a reward for his information and his skill as a healer. It was never, however, part

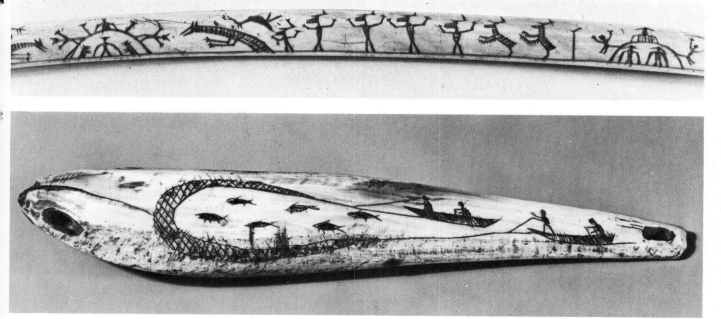

50 **Spoon carved from a walrus's shoulder joint,** engraved with hunting scenes. (6 cm wide). From the Canadian arctic, 20th century. (Staatliches Museum für Völkerkunde, Munich)

51 **Ivory bow drill** engraved with a scene of a shaman in his hut charming caribou spirits for the hunters. Probably from the Canadian arctic, 19th century. (Museum of Mankind, London)

52 **Ivory net weight** in the form of a fish, engraved with a scene of fishing with a seine net. Probably from the Canadian arctic, early 19th century. (James Hooper Collection)

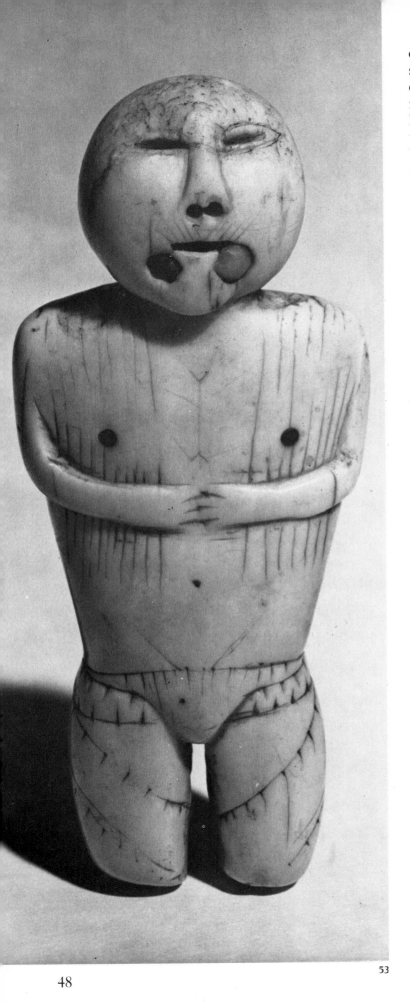

of Eskimo ethics to respect wealth and even a rich shaman would feel it incumbent upon him occasionally to distribute his wealth among the neighbours. The angakoq, as he was usually called, had a considerable influence upon art. Even when he was not a carver himself, his descriptions of the spirit beings whom he encountered were of great importance to the artists in the community. His personal equipment also was much ornamented with carvings. In some areas of Alaska the angakoq wore a painted wooden mask, related to those used by the neighbouring Indian groups, though in the use of pale colour and long elegant outlines the Eskimo tradition was strongly marked. In northern Alaska a few 'frame' masks still survived, in which the angakoq surrounded his face with figures and symbols in a framework. His equipment also included cases for catching spirits who were to be banished, pendant animal shapes to aid his skill in making contact with the souls of the creatures, and ornaments for his magic drum. The angakoq was by no means a political power among the Eskimos; he was just a person endowed with special powers, which often made him rather unfitted to be a great hunter or a leader of men. His frequent dissociation of personality made him unreliable in the ordinary sense. Nevertheless, the community would be greatly inconvenienced without the presence of its seer and prophet. Women could achieve eminence in the field of magic, though they were less common than men in the groups of shamans who would meet if opportunity offered. Like the men, they carried their little bags of magical objects, often ivory and wood carvings representing spirits, and usually some false fangs which could be slipped into the mouth and extruded to add to the audience's impression that their shaman was possessed by some strange animal spirit while in trance. It would never do for an angakoq to fail to produce phenomena, and therefore all were prepared to use straightforward conjuring tricks to impress their audience. However, many instances are recorded of shamans predicting events, divining the presence of lost property, and of dreaming true visions. They were not usually people who suddenly decided they were possessed by spirits. Normally the young angakoq went to a learned specialist and studied the arts of drumming himself into a trance state, and of contacting the spirit powers. Fees were paid in kind, and the junior became a veritable sorcerer's apprentice, serving the master with devotion, assisting both in the meditations and in the manufacture of impressive phenomena.

The angakoq was not unique in Eskimo society, since any member of a community might receive messages from the spirit world. On the whole, people

53

54

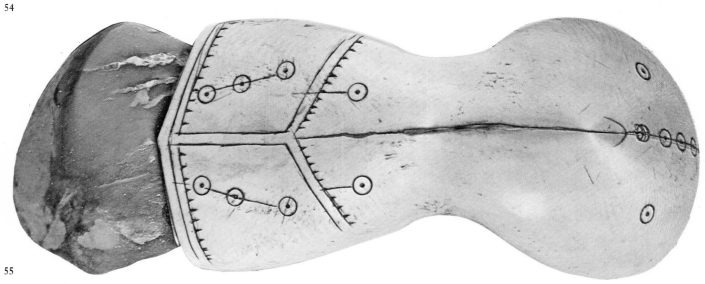

55

55

53 **Shaman's charm.** A human figure of ivory inlaid with stones
    (13 cm high). From Banks Island, Alaska, 1800–1880. (Museum of
    the American Indian, New York)

54 **Mythological giant owl.** Green stone. From the Canadian arctic,
    20th century. (Gimpel Collection)

55 **Jade scraper** used as an adze for preparing the surface of wood.
    The grip has been shaped to fit the fingers of the carver. Mammoth
    ivory haft. Probably from the Canadian arctic, 19th century.
    (Museum of Mankind, London)

56 Wooden dance mask with features of man and seal, painted green, red and white. In shamanistic performances the heads of spirit beings are often seen emerging from the mouth of the shaman. From Alaska, late 19th century. (American Museum of Natural History, New York)

57 Wooden paddle painted with scenes of a walrus hunt. From Alaska, late 19th century. (Museum of Mankind, London)

56

were afraid of the recently dead, and a great deal of trouble was taken to ensure that a relative died away from the home if possible. This might well lead to a speeding up of death, but all the same it is clear that the Eskimos were a kindly, affectionate people and cared for the sick and old until the end became inevitable. Well after death the spirit was thought to have a care of relatives, and to dream of the dead was an indication of their interest. To see visions of dead relatives was frightening, but sometimes such apparitions were indications which helped the hunter in the pursuit of game. In general, the ghostly visitation was thought of as either good advice for the hunter, or as a warning which must be heeded. It may well be that most of these visions arose from the inner personality of the individual seeing the vision, but they were accepted as real occurrences deriving from other living beings.

Every Eskimo had some personal spirit protector. It often took animal form, and was acquired in late childhood through some circumstance in which the animal appeared to help. There were initiation ceremonies for youngsters but they were not like the ordeals of loneliness undertaken by the American Indians to the south. The reason was that the arctic terrain usually meant that a lone journey in search of inspiration would result in death. In the Alaskan area the onset of puberty would mean that the boy would separate from his family and find a sleeping place in the communal house used for group activities in the settlement. In other regions there were ceremonies and some segregation. Girls were universally separated from the group for their first two menstrual periods. The ceremonial separation was a signal to the community that the girl was marriageable and that her parents would welcome enquiries with a view to marriage. These rites of passage from childhood to adult status were important though not marked by the ceremonialism of more favoured regions of the earth. Vitality, sex and procreation were linked as a kind of spiritual development. The dreams and visions natural to the period were taken to be the advice of the spirit world, and it was hoped that the ancestors would be concerned. In many communities it was the custom to name the newest baby after the last deceased member of the community, and there was said to be a spiritual bond between them, though reincarnation was never a formalised belief.

Of course all living beings had souls, both men and animals. One soul was immanent in the body, directed all living action and continued the thought of the person throughout life. At death it usually faded away to be replaced by its duplicate which had been present all the time but began a really independent existence at death. Any person might become separated from his soul in illness, when the shaman would be called in to capture the wandering spirit and return it to its proper body. But also any person might dissociate in sleep so that the spirit could visit the place of the ancestors or the realms of the animals and return to the body when awakening. The information obtained in the dream, if remembered, would influence the conduct of daily life as if it were a real waking experience. Experience of the supernatural was common, a phenomenon which perhaps could be expected under the circumstances of arctic life. The separation of the hunt and its excitement for the men was equalled by the importance of the work around the house felt by the women who were always busy and always a little anxious. The mysterious advent of storm or fog passed across the people and no one was quite sure whether the apparent was quite real. The idea of enchanters who took the forms of seals to delude the hunter, or of sea spirits who lured young men to their doom, was as real to the Eskimos as to any medieval European peasant; only to the Eskimos these events might occur in reality at any time.

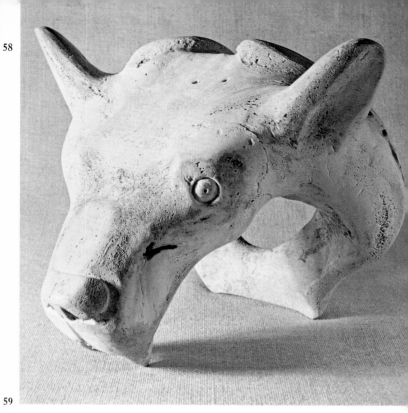
58

59
60

58 Good spirit by Manasie Manaipik. The carving conveys the idea of a dual personality in one body. Whale vertebrae ($32 \times 48 \times 19$ cm). Pangnirtung, N.W.T., 1969. (Collection: Macmillan–Bloedel Limited, Vancouver, B.C.)

59–60 Bear spirit (back and front views). The human face on the back is the feminine one of a pair of heads. Whale vertebrae. From the Canadian arctic, 20th century. (Gimpel Collection)

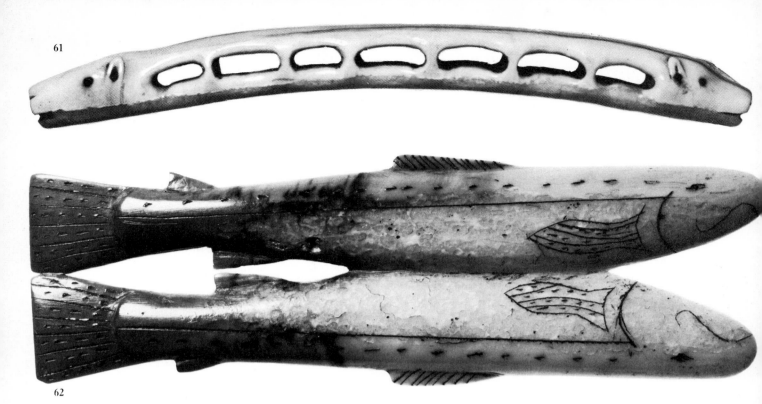

61

62

63

61 **Dog harness terret** carved with dogs' heads. (The terret separates the reins of the dog team). Walrus ivory (14 cm long). Western Eskimo. Acquired 1903. (Royal Scottish Museum, Edinburgh)
62 **Handle** carved as two conjoined fish. Used as a grip to hold a seal or fish line. Walrus ivory (11 cm long). From Nunivak Island, Alaska. Acquired 1957. (Royal Scottish Museum, Edinburgh)
63 **Eye-shade.** Birch wood and walrus tooth, stitched with baleen. Aleut, mid 19th century. (Museum of Mankind, London)
64 Group of ivories: **Walrus ivory snow knife** depicting a whale and walrus hunt; **Harpoon rest from a kayak**; **Two toggles** in the form of seals; **Fishermen's charms**, used to divine the outcome of an expedition. All from Alaska, 19th century. (Museum of Mankind, London)

The Eskimos expressed their practical and spiritual attitude to life in their involvement with ivory carvings and bone sculptures which combined usefulness with magic powers. There was usually no point in trying to make a large sculpture. It had no functional use. The angakoq might need a mask for ceremonies, or perhaps a tusk carved with little masks which represented the spirit world, but the ordinary hunter needed harpoon heads, toggles for affixing his weapons to the kayak or sledge, little fasteners for sealing floats, and wound plugs to stop up the weapon holes in slain seals so that the bodies could be towed behind the kayak. There were also toggles for fixing carrying straps for dragging home the game. Dog traces, too, had ivory fastening buttons.

Most of the work of making these things was done in the winter months when game was scarce and the daylight was gone. Then in between occasional festal gatherings of the community, the men would carve and polish the things they needed for life. Their tools were of the simplest, and a century ago were still mainly of flaked stone. Each object was scraped into shape and then abraded to final form and polished. The later Eskimos were more interested in smooth surfaces than the Dorset people who were their ancestors. So they spent a good deal of time abrading the surfaces with whatever stone was available and then gently polishing with fat and their hands. It took a lot of time, but an object when carved was improved by handling and fondling from time to time. It made a kind of personal contact, and produced a form of beauty which was appreciated by the family. A wife was as proud of her husband's tools as he was proud

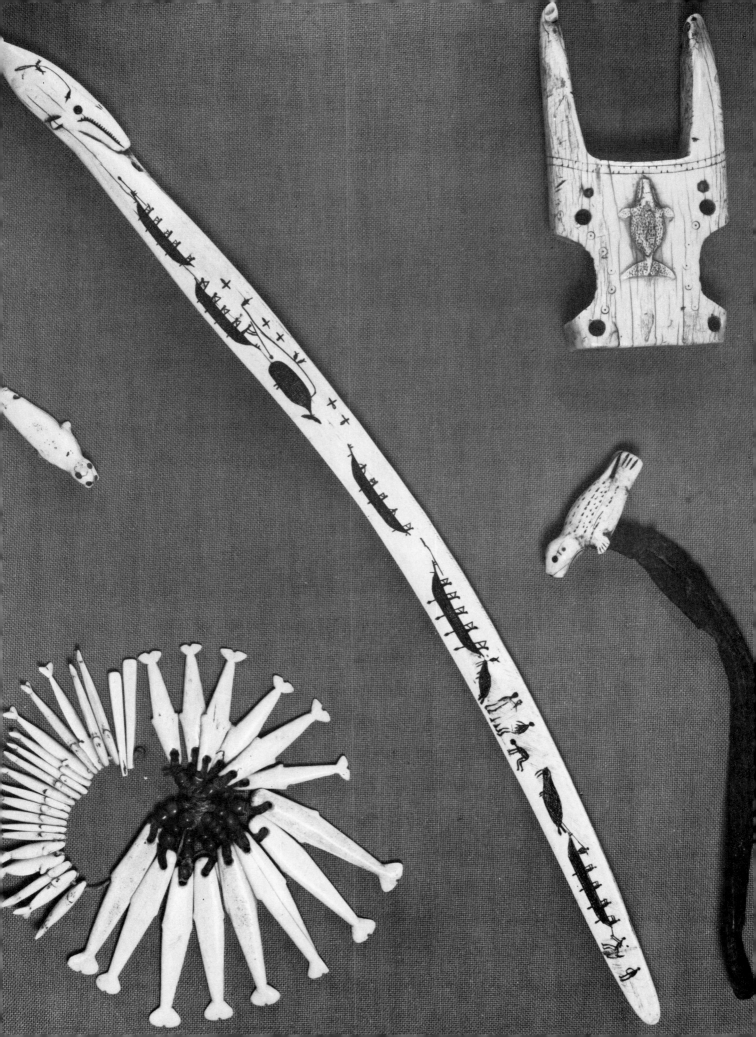

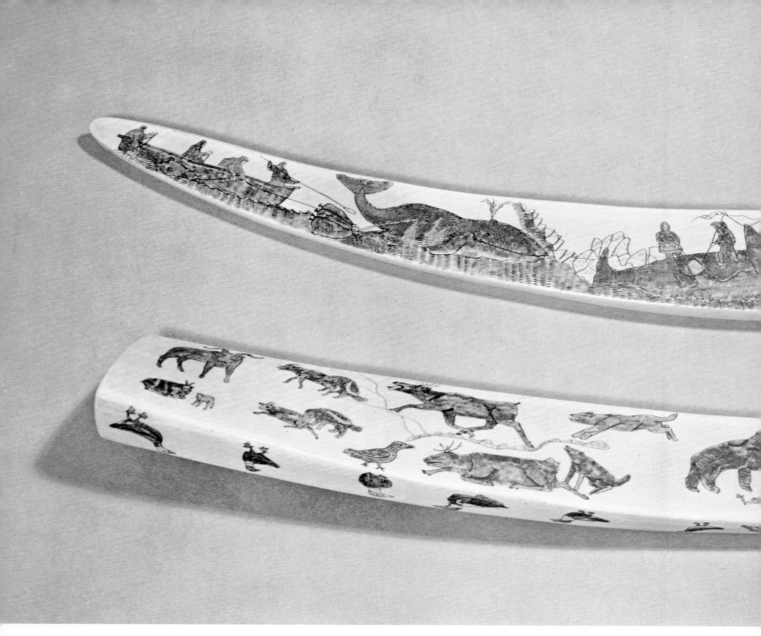

of the fine fur clothes which she made for him. In turn he made her a needle-case, and thimbles. Anything at all might take on an animal form or present a surface for decoration. The beauty of form and colour was appreciated in the community, but suitability for the purpose of practical use was the real point. It was a matter for the artist personally to choose whether the form he used represented a protective spirit being. It might be a bear or a fox, or a bird; all might be helpers of human hunters who were in spiritual contact through the world of souls. Hence we find much in the practical arts of everyday life that has a real quality of life within it. It is also invariably easy and pleasant to handle in use. Simplified forms were important because most of the toggles, harpoons, and spear-throwers were handled in practice under conditions where the hands could not be bare for fear of frost bite. Everything must be smooth and easy to guide into place.

Indoors the simplest things were shaped for use

and so acquired beauty. Simple net gauges and netting needles were rarely decorated beyond a few incised lines, but they were well placed and acceptable. Implements such as handled flaking tools for the blade maker were fitted with plain or carved handles of good shape. Combs were important articles of adornment as well as cleanliness, so the flat surface above the teeth formed an area which had been beautified from the earliest times. Eskimo forms included outline figures and scrimshaw scenes. The subjects usually conveyed to the artist the idea of good fortune. Powerful tools, such as the perforated ivory levers which were used as arrow straighteners, were carved with fortunate symbols of the quarry the arrow was expected to bring down. Among these, seals, polar bears, and caribou were most important. Sometimes, as in Palaeolithic Europe, the whole object represented the desired animal; sometimes just the head of the animal was represented, and the body of the instrument was engraved with magical themes.

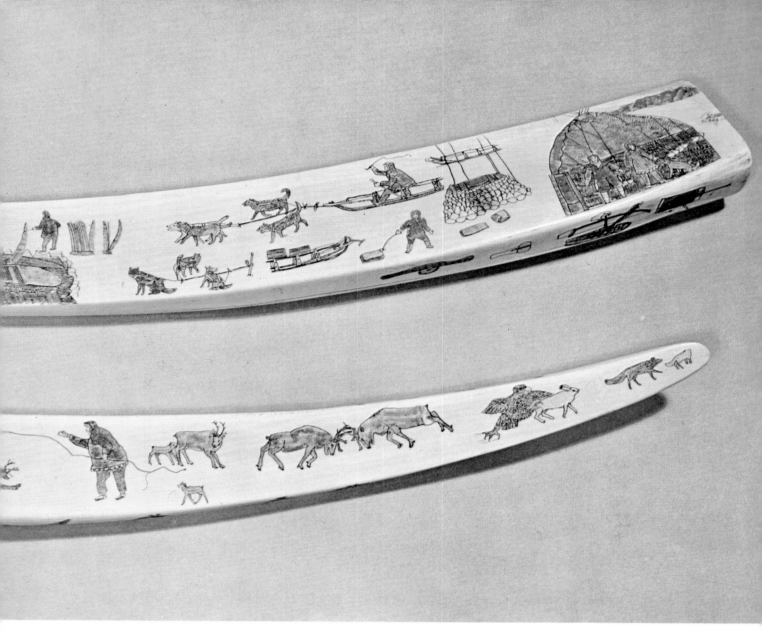

In some of them we find pictures of magic in which magicians turn into caribou, or caribou spirits become birds. They are strange but direct pictorial works which stem from an absolute acceptance of the beliefs they illustrate.

Women were involved in the arts quite as naturally as men. They might paint pieces of woodwork, or make a kind of embroidered leather stitchery on their needlecase flaps. Each woman made clothes for her family according to the local fashion, and she chose furs which were not only practical but of colours and tones to make decorative borders to the garments. Sometimes she added short fringes of skin, or pendant strings of fish vertebrae. The results were often of great beauty. Styles varied from place to place and the two sexes had differing costume, but it was an honour to a woman that her menfolk were splendidly dressed in efficient hunting costumes as well as in outfits for life in the village where they might be present at community dances. For themselves, the women spent even more time on wearing the most elegant of fashion in clothing. Styles differed from area to area, but in each place the quality of the sewing and the choice of furs was of great importance. Since they were less outdoors than the men, they were able to indulge in some coquetry. In Greenland the areas between the top of the long boots and short trousers were often left bare so that the soft brown thighs could be seen. In harsh conditions little wraps of white fur covered the bare patches. Elsewhere the jacket was deeply scooped out at the sides so that an area of midriff above the hipster trousers was left bare to emphasise physical attractiveness. The great hoods in which the babies were carried could be adjusted to show a glimpse of bare shoulder, and faces, often strangely beautiful, were decorated with

65 **Walrus tusks** engraved and tinted with hunting and whaling scenes. Siberian Eskimo, late 19th century. (Collection: Hudson's Bay Company)

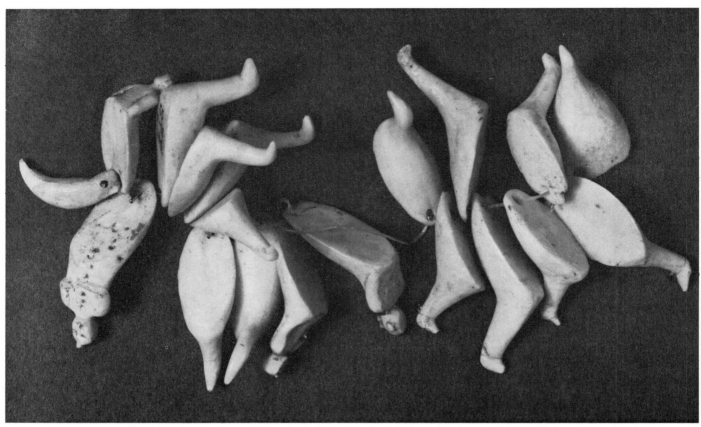

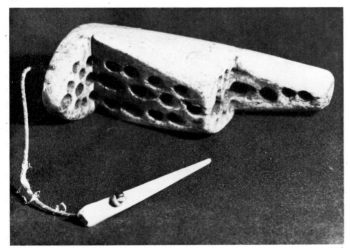

66 **Needlecase** of walrus ivory engraved with hunting scenes
blackened with soot. Note the rare depiction of a tree. From
Alaska. Acquired 1901. (Royal Scottish Museum, Edinburgh)

67 **Ivory gambling counters,** including geese, swans and mermaids.
19th century. (Museum of Mankind, London)

68 **Ajegaung,** an Eskimo game in which the object is to jerk the peg
so that it falls into one of the holes. Whale bone (10.5 cm long,
peg 7.5 cm). Baffin Island, 1911. (Anthropological Museum,
University of Aberdeen)

lines of tattooed dots across the cheeks or below the
lips.

Indoors, in the heavily insulated and overheated
winter houses, whether of stone or wood or snow
blocks, most of the old-time Eskimos went naked.
In parts of Alaska tiny cache-sexe hip strings were
used by men, though rarely. In Greenland the girls
often wore a tiny cover for their pudenda, but this was
as much an ornament as an adjunct of modesty.
It was very elegantly embroidered and many
specimens were decorated with pendant chains of
fish spines. However, clothing was rare for indoor
occasions, and sexual behaviour was natural so that
Western ideas of decency or taboos of the body were
not of any importance until the days of close contact
with Europeans and religious missions. But it should
be noted that the introduction of different houses had
more effect on outward modesty indoors than any
change of belief.

Sex was not overtly expressed in art except for
objects associated with some of the festivals for the
changing of the seasons, particularly those before the
hunts began, for then it was important to bring nature

58

into a creative mood, so that animals might more freely copulate with fruitful results. In Alaska in old times there was a spring festival in which young men wore masks and carried around bone or ivory penes strapped to their bodies, but this was rare.

Many of the little naked ivory figures of men and women are simple and modest in nature. They were often used as charms to be put under a woman's pillow so that her children should be beautiful. The sex of the figure was meant to indicate the desired sex of the baby to come.

Life was all of a unity to the Eskimos. Women were quite as important as men except that too many girl babies were sometimes a liability since they would not grow up to be hunters. But the balance of work within the family was nicely adjusted to the relative strengths and temperaments of the two sexes. On the whole the occupations in and around the home were those for women, and the hunting and journeying were those for men. But this is only seen in art in the design of clothing. Early carved human figures rarely showed people at work, though the introduction of the art of scrimshaw was the occasion of many linear pictures of everyday life. Here the themes are mainly factual, and the sexual elements are rare, though they occurred sometimes with magical connotations.

When we consider all the objects of an Eskimo household, it is clear that the production of works of art did not take up a very large place. It was an adjunct to the useful arts, and was mainly a product of life through the terrible winter night. The purposes were usually strictly practical, even when magical, and the only really specialised artistic output came with the masks and objects used in the shamanistic performance of the angakoq.

An important aspect of early Eskimo art was the play element. A great many pieces of ivory were carved into birds and animals which rose up from a flat base rather like pictures of ducks omitting all parts below the water line. They were usually of thumb-nail size, often ornamented with patterns of lines and dots, and really most attractive. Their purpose was simply to be used as gambling counters. A handful of the little objects was thrown down on to a skin mat or anything handy, and the value of the throw was determined by the number which fell right way up and those which fell on their side. Games went on for long periods to while away the tedium of the arctic evenings. Great fortunes were not won or lost, though some people became compulsive gamblers. But in a small closed community of Eskimos, all deeply committed to the sharing out of wealth, gambling was not a great problem; it was fun of a fascinating kind. Because it was so popular, the pieces were usually

made with care, and skill was displayed on them. To some extent they were status symbols, for the good craftsman was always respected.

Another very popular pastime which had a great influence on art was the ubiquitous cat's cradle, in which a piece of thong was turned around the fingers to make an outline representation of some object. The designs made were numerous, and usually traditional. Sometimes the strings went only around the fingers, at others fingers and toes were used. Naturally, skill at the game started in childhood, but it was never abandoned, and as life went on skill became more developed, until in old age it would be a delight to teach the grandchildren, and often mystify them by clever development of unsuspected designs. The patterns produced by the criss-crossing strings were not always realistic, but their meaning was instantly recognised by the family in the tent or snow house. The cat's cradle was often chosen to tell a story, starting with a loose loop around the fingers, and building ever more intricate symbolic pictures which illustrated the objects described as the story progressed. A simple myth, like the story of the hunter who chased with his dog team as far as the place where earth met the sky and who can still be seen chasing along as Ursa Major among the stars, was well suited to the string-figure technique. The process of the attachment of realistic interpretation to abstract forms was not a conscious one, but just a natural consequence of the game, but here again there was room for a highly individual interpretation of any abstract form which might evoke one of the figures in the string game. Mostly to the Eskimos the game was the occasion for delighted laughter as one figure followed another on the fingers of a skilled player.

Laughter seems to have been an important characteristic of Eskimo life. Most travellers who stayed with Eskimos noted the child-like glee with which any good fortune or new friendship were welcomed. These people, always living on the icy edge of life or death, were not depressed. There was always something to do, and something to sing over as they worked. Work was hard and often incredibly difficult. Think of the woman chewing a boot sole before making each stitch with her bone needle, or the man sitting for hours beside a seal blow-hole before the time came to make the fatal stroke. To a people living in such a world as the arctic, emotional life was a succession of quiet waiting and exhilarating success. A way of life quite alien to the clean and civilised European brought happiness to the Eskimos. Happiness was enhanced by personal prowess. For the men a reputation as a good hunter or a skilled craftsman was a very satisfying achievement. It was

69

70

also very important in the small community, usually of less than fifty individuals, to be able to come to the dance in the community house well dressed in fine clothes. The display of fine things in company, and the ability to give fine presents of food to neighbours because of good hunting, were much prized. In the circle of the winter house where three or four families might live together, industry at work and pleasantness when playing or talking made the cramped conditions bearable. The indoor nakedness led to admiration of physical fitness, and some delight in good tattooing, and it also played a part in the gentle natural forms

of much Eskimo art. Life, humanity and magic were all combined naturally in the traditional art of the arctic people.

69 Ivories: **Standing man** ($5 \times 2.5 \times 1$ cm); **Standing woman** ($21.8 \times 1.5 \times 1$ cm; **Man in kayak** ($3 \times 15 \times 2.5$ cm). Possibly from the east coast of Labrador, pre 1914. (National Museum of Man, Ottawa)

70 **Woodcut** showing an Eskimo waiting at a blow hole, unaware that a monster is creeping up on him. From an Eskimo book called Gronlandske Folkesagn, 1860. From southern Greenland. (Museum of Mankind, London)

71 **Mother and Child.** Black stone and sealskin ($31 \times 21 \times 19$ cm). Port Harrison, Quebec, 1957. (National Museum of Man, Ottawa)

Modern Times

The nineteenth century began the change; by its end many Eskimos owned guns for hunting, and whole families had travelled on whaling ships and accepted wages mostly in clothing and storage foods. They had begun to congregate at settlements where there was contact with the white men which made up for restrictions in hunting. The continuing improvement of climate had opened more of the arctic to the whales, with the consequent advance of whalers. An unforeseen consequence of contact was the spread of new diseases; venereal diseases became widespread, and smallpox was a scourge, but most terrible of all was the common cold which choked thousands of non-immune victims to death. Governments sent doctors where possible who replaced the primitive medicines of the angakoq. Religious bodies sent out more Christian missionaries who replaced the magic, but did not extirpate the many charming stories of native folklore. Thus, at the beginning of the twentieth century, the forces of change in the arctic were strong and gathering momentum. The Eskimos were everywhere faced with a problem of dwindling food-animals, and of the gradual exchange of hunting for fur trapping. With new wooden houses, woollen trade garments and wooden boats, they were finding some compensation for the loss of the late Stone Age type of life that their ancestors had enjoyed. Life was becoming more strange to the elders, but the younger folk were finding it quite attractive, especially the opportunities of living in larger communities with more human contacts.

Culturally the impact of the technological world has not yet destroyed Eskimo life, but it has altered the framework within which a few families continue to live in the old way but where most have adopted a mixed culture.

For the white man there was a similar rapid change. The old sailing ship was now a steamer. Education had become compulsory, and the great commercial companies spread their search for raw materials much further. The internal combustion engine began to replace the horse; airships lifted into the air, and in 1902 the first aeroplane flew a little way. And, in the north, governments began to realise that they had more responsibility than they imagined for the welfare of the people of the arctic.

Greenland Eskimos, at least in the south and east, made steady progress. They had their close ties with Denmark through the official Trading Company. The missionaries, following up the early work of Hans Egede, were running modern schools, and the people gradually came to live in well-designed wooden houses. The trading contacts were steady, and many families made a living from trapping animals and from sealing and fishing for an export market. Their clothing altered in fashion, not towards European styles, but to a variant of practical arctic clothing of which much consisted of imported woollens. Many spare-time carvers produced ivory carvings for sale, knowing that they would go to Denmark to earn money for their families. A few Danish families living in Greenland established some cattle farming, and Eskimo helpers slowly learned the arts of conserving animal stock for breeding and not for hunting. Change was very slow, and not at all easy for the older people to accept, but it was a change that the Eskimos desired. They were becoming a civilised people in the modern world. Already they could read and write, and a few of their artists became well known as illustrators. But it is to be noted that the slow development of the southern Greenlanders was basically in an Eskimo direction. The kayaks and throwing boards, the eye-shades and summer tents had all remained part of their culture. The arctic adaptations to life were not subverted but simply grew to be parts of a new way of life which more and more tended to exist in small townships of wooden dwellings. The Eskimos had become part of the peoples of the North Atlantic seaboard. Their close ties with Denmark became natural links rather than symbols of domination, and this was due to the common sense and friendly procedures of officials and state trading enterprises.

In the first decade of this century the Greenlanders became aware of their distant cousins, the people of the polar north who were still living in very primitive conditions isolated from the rest of the world at the north western angle of the country. Although their

---

72 Head and torso of a bear emerging from the sea by Amidilak. Black stone and ivory (17.5 × 11 × 14 cm). Port Harrison, Quebec, 1953. (Canadian Guild of Crafts – Quebec Branch, Montreal)

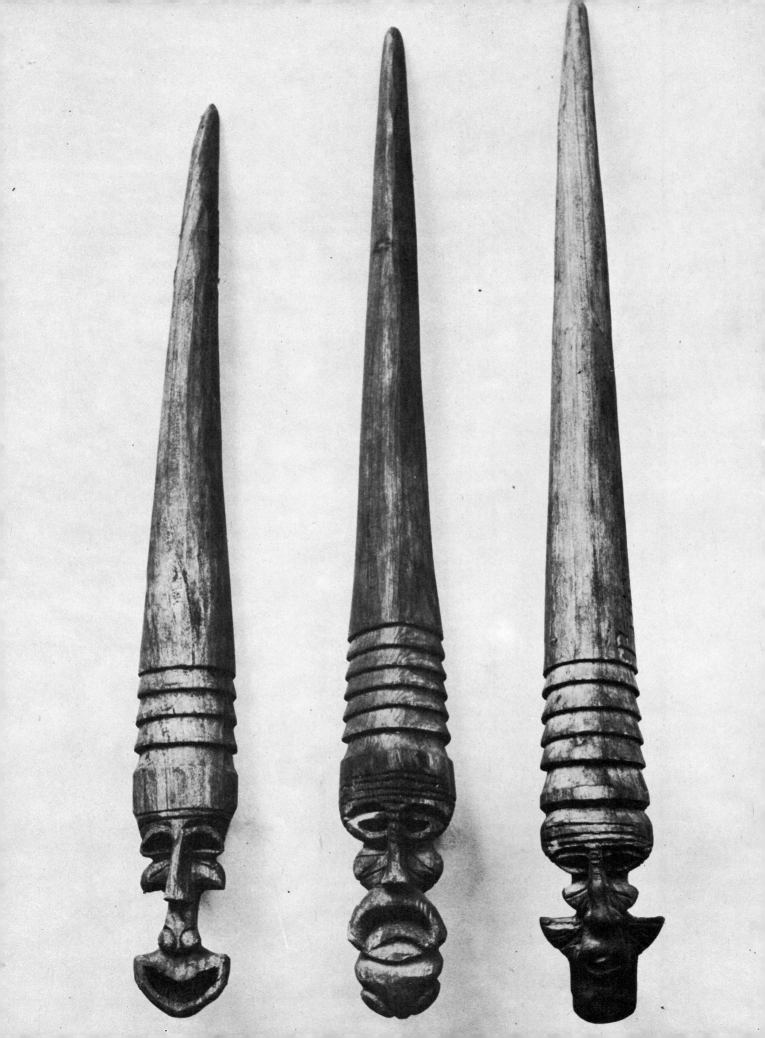

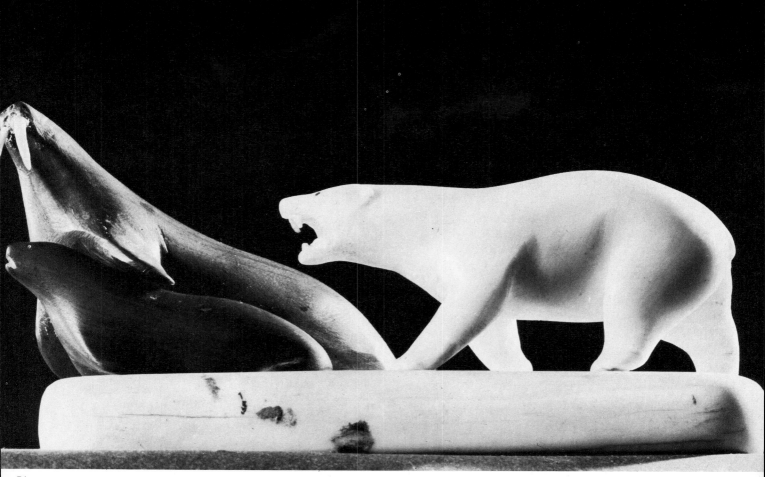

74

primitive type of Thule culture had been influenced
by contact with the migrants from the Canadian arctic
in the 1860s, they were still living in the ancient way,
supporting themselves in all things by ice hunting.

The development of a new trade-oriented way of
life could not follow the same direction in the far north
as it had in south and east Greenland. Conditions
were far too harsh. Not many European or American
products were of immediate value to the people near
the pole. Guns for hunting were the most acceptable
change. But no framed house or organised schooling
was of much use. They were compelled to live in
stone-built huts and in the snow domes when ice
hunting. Everyone, including the children, was
involved in the struggle to win life from the frozen
wastes of the far north.

In 1950 Greenland was changed in political status.
It became an integral part of Denmark, and all
Greenlanders became Danish citizens. The change
helped to unify all the trading developments and the
spread of education. More funds became available for
the slow work of acculturation. Under these
conditions, art among the Eskimo population was
encouraged as a spare-time activity, and there was
some increase in its economic value to the people.
For the polar north, the NATO base at Thule was
a most important change. The Polar Eskimos never
numbered more than a few hundred individuals; now

75

73 **Wooden throat plugs with carved faces.** When a seal is killed,
its lungs are deflated and a plug is inserted into the windpipe so that
it can be more easily towed behind the kayak. The plugs also act
as good luck charms. (Longest 26.3 cm). From Angmagssalik,
Greenland. Collected 1931. (Danish National Museum,
Copenhagen)

74 **Polar bear attacking walrus with young** by Kulaut. Walrus
tusk and steatite (12.7 cm long). Igloolik, N.W.T., 1954.
(Collection: Jørgen Meldgaard, Copenhagen)

75 **Tupilak.** A dangerous spirit who haunts the ice and brings
disaster to hunters and misfortune to anyone who meets him.
Wood. From Angmagssalik, Greenland, late 19th–early 20th
century. (Danish National Museum, Copenhagen)

they were in the midst of activities which had not even entered their dreams. It is to the credit of their way of life that they were able to accept, as a natural event, the intrusion of a technological world in advance of that known in many civilised countries. They were food providers to the base, and then labourers. Many became skilled technicians, obtaining work of sufficiently good standing to enable them to purchase housing and packaged foods for the support of their families. The cultural revolution was thrust upon the Polar Eskimos in a few years instead of a few generations. For the carvers there was a new market, but really it was of small importance, especially since the Polar Eskimos had previously led so hard a life that there was little time for any experiment in the finer aspects of art. Carvings were made but they were simple and strong rather than elegant; perhaps one could describe them as nearer to the ancient Dorset art than the developed Thule style which was ancestral to modern Eskimo art.

On the western side of the Eskimo world, the progress was not unlike that on the east. However, the growth of an artistic culture had an earlier beginning because of trade contacts. The Siberian Eskimos have become citizens of the U.S.S.R. and, being in direct contact with the state through their local councils and co-operatives, they have been able to form part of the cultural life of the country without giving up their basic subsistence activities. Education and schooling had been among them for a long time, and they were fully ready to enter the modern world. The change for them has also been great but not total.

The purchase of Alaska from Russia altered the balance of contact for the Aleuts. More missionaries came, and gradually, as policy towards native peoples became more enlightened, the Aleuts found themselves provided with schools and teachers. Their relationship to the fishing industries was of great importance and has brought them into the world of trade. American fishery companies have been in close contact with the Aleuts and the result has been an improvement in their standard of living. There was some attempt to establish reservations to protect the native people on some of the islands, but most of the Aleuts have been able to work on equal terms with the other settlers in their islands. The old ways have been disappearing ever more rapidly, and the ancient works of art are as much fascinating curiosities to the modern Aleut as to the Americans. In the process of acculturation, the Aleuts have made some very attractive models of their skin boats with crews and full equipment, and a number of ivory carvings of scenes of everyday life in ivory of quite astonishing whiteness. However, this has developed more as a curio market than an entry to the realms of fine art.

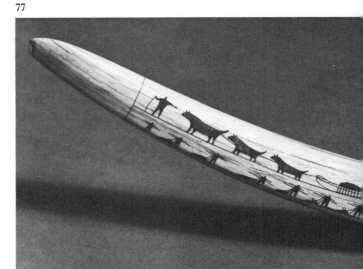

We have had to look at the Aleuts as separate from the Eskimos of Alaska because of the linguistic division and the differences which their all the year round sea fishing activities have highlighted.

The contacts of the Alaskan Eskimos among European explorers and sailors gave them some idea of the larger world outside, and they learned to make very good engravings on ivory which often went beyond the usual limits of scrimshaw work. However, the main effect of the contact was not to produce art, but fish and skins. Some people served with the whalers on ships, others came to trading posts, bringing supplies of dried fish and meat to trade for the desirable things of the white man. They needed guns, knives, and canvas most of all. It was all very wonderful that these things from the foreigners helped them to catch more game, and to hunt successfully. The hunters gradually learned that the arctic mammals were not only important from the Eskimo point of view for food and clothing but that

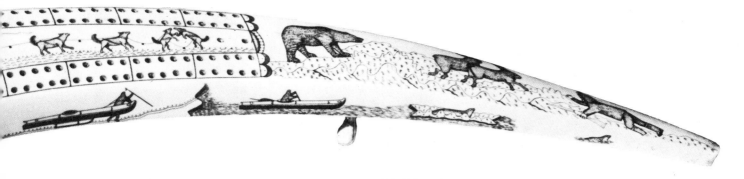

76 **Cribbage board** with realistic engravings. The Eskimos learned to make cribbage boards from contacts with whalers in the mid 19th century and the gold rushes stimulated the sale of ivory carving. The finest cribbage boards were those made around the turn of the century. From the Nome area, Alaska, about 1905. (University of Alaska Museum, College, Alaska)

77 **Walrus tusk** engraved with hunting and housebuilding scenes. From Alaska. Acquired 1909. (Horniman Museum, London)

trade in furs could bring in more useful goods. Before the 1890s, most Siberian Eskimos had learned the use of traps and lines of snares. They had entered into the fur trade without thinking of the scarcities which would ensue a generation ahead.

They did not realise either that now a new people laid claim to their land. The Americans were now feeling a responsibility towards the native peoples of their lands and gradually encouraged the spread of knowledge even if it was given only through mission schools.

Then came catastrophe. Gold was discovered in the Yukon. The gold rush brought in great numbers of rough settlers, miners, business people, saloons and food shops. The Eskimos met the white man on bad terms and found more misery than profit from the trade in skin clothing and in women. Eventually the gold rush petered out. Ruined towns survived here and there, and stretches of unused road cut into the hills. Some whites lived in the settlements around the coast. There were many young people who were neither white nor Eskimo, and there arose a good deal of racial intolerance. However, many of the whites were interested in the Eskimos and some continued to live as pioneers in the lonely north where they really tried to help the local people on the path to a more adequate life.

As time went on the government took an increasing interest in Eskimo education. Hundreds of girls and boys learned to read and write in English. They also spent time in drawing. Half the school time was wisely spent in teaching Eskimo crafts so that when the children grew up they would not be totally out of touch with the life of their people. They were subjected to all manner of aptitude and intelligence tests in which they tended to achieve higher marks early on and then gradually declined to a level below that of the local white children as they grew older. Of course the white children came from homes with a totally different outlook.

The educational programme was urgent because of the development of trading posts and fish canneries along the rich Alaskan west coast. There were jobs to be filled, community relations to be encouraged and a whole group of tribespeople to be gradually integrated into the ways of the civilised Americans. Alaska without gold was still a rich country, and the canneries became famous all over the world. Many Eskimos found useful employment in the new industry. Those who were free remained as trappers with a bias towards hunting for basic family subsistence. But more time was available and more new ideas were circulating.

Missionaries of many sects worked among the Eskimos, usually helpfully. However, the gradual change to Christianity led to emphasis on the nuclear family, and the old communal houses in which the young men found shelter and all the people met for dances and traditional story telling gradually fell out of use. Even the traditional folk tales of the Eskimos began to assimilate other themes from the white teachers. There was also a small but steady trade down the west coast in Eskimo curios; ivory and soapstone carvings, dolls, and models of Eskimo life which had a market value. This was never a deliberate policy; it simply developed as a by-product of the culture contact between the two peoples.

By 1930 education had progressed; some Eskimos had even gone to college and travelled by aeroplane. But world events were to cause further changes, later on. The world balance of power demanded a defence line of radar stations right across the arctic. In Alaska as well as in Greenland the Eskimos found that they could become skilled technicians and enjoy a higher social status. Alaska became a fully fledged State, and with this change there was a heightened interest in the welfare of the natives. The most recent great change in Alaska has been the discovery of an enormously rich oil-field near the shores of the Arctic Ocean. Again Eskimos have been engaged as workers and professional hunters. So they have found a higher standard of living, though in a manner hardly dreamed of by their parents. However, the construction of pipe lines has interfered with the migrations of the caribou, and special arrangements have had to be made to help those Eskimo groups whose livelihood is threatened. All in all we may say that the Alaskan Eskimos were the most advanced people of their race in old times, and that the change of climate as well as the greater cultural exchanges have kept them in the forefront of development.

The story of the Eskimos living in the Canadian arctic is far more complicated. There were fewer of them, some 15,000 out of a total Eskimo population of about 80,000. In culture they differed widely from one another because of the variety of natural resources and also because of the great distances between one group and another. The arctic explorers had found them a cheerful people who were always ready to welcome visitors, and who faced life on the edge of disaster with patience and a spirit of hopefulness. They relied a great deal on their belief that the great mother spirit living under the sea would send her children, the seals and whales, to help her human protégés. The spirits in the air were also ever around. When disaster struck, people died, sometimes a whole community. That was natural, and was perhaps aided by evil magic. But for the good hunter and the well-organised family, life brought enough and left a little time over for enjoyment and social life within the small communities of a few dozen people. Sometimes, though rarely, they met strangers and that was the occasion for an orgy of happiness and friendship. Food, companionship, sex, and a general sense of cosiness made life totally enjoyable on such occasions. But everybody knew well enough that the food animals were limited and that the visitors would return to their own group when the time came, in order to spare the food supplies of their hosts. The pleasant days of summer passed, and with happy memories and tales to tell by the winter blubber lamps they returned, hunting as they went.

The Eskimos who were most remote from the normal way of life were the Caribou Eskimos of Keewatin. These people lived like late Palaeolithic hunters of the last Ice Age. Fortunately for our understanding they were sought out in the early part of the twentieth century by Canadian ethnologists who have given us a very full series of studies of their way of life. It was fortunate also for the Caribou Eskimos because they were now known to the Canadian authorities, and visited occasionally.

Disaster struck the Caribou Eskimos in the middle of the century; epidemics of respiratory diseases broke out and took a terrible toll, and nearly a third of their small population died. Then a scarcity of caribou developed. Disease had also struck the herds, and there had also been dispersal through hunting, so smaller groups passed over the usual migration routes. The Canadian authorities had established some welfare help but the Eskimos with typical self reliance failed to send word of the extreme economic difficulties which threatened them. They tried fishing through the ice with little effect. The bands tried to keep apart on the good old tradition of allowing each as much hunting ground as possible. But one group suffered a greater disaster. An accidental fire in a store hut burned it down, killed two of the men working at it, and caused the death by starvation of seventeen other isolated people. That single disaster nearly

destroyed a hunting group, and with the whole of the Caribou Eskimo population down to less than 500 individuals the loss seemed critical. News of the tragedy of these remote people lifted them out of the world of romantic imagining. They were very real, and very much in trouble.

Should the Caribou Eskimos be rescued and brought together into a village in a warmer climate where they could be taught handicrafts and earn a living and independence in new surroundings? That was proposed to the Eskimos, but they were against it. The men who were leaders in each little band voiced the thoughts of the people who felt that this land was their spiritual home. They would not allow themselves to go away from the beautiful world of their people. Strangers might see it as a terrible wilderness, but to them it was a living world in which the spirits were close to humans.

Another more real danger faced them. They were helped with supplies and houses. As far as possible groups were persuaded to come together, but the result was a group of tiny settlements with no means of subsistence, for the hunting remained too poor to support the hunters. They might well have become wards of the State living off doles of food and clothing and losing all their initiative. Eventually the groups

78 Rookery. The cliff is made of core ivory from the socket end of a walrus tusk. It is spattered with paint representing the birds' droppings. The birds perched on the cliff are murres, puffins and a cormorant. The base is of polished ivory. (20.5 cm high). From St. Lawrence Island, Bering Sea, about 1945. (University of Alaska Museum, College, Alaska)

were persuaded to settle at least for the winter at
Baker Lake, where there would be shelter and a
certainty of food during the harsh days. It was in the
Baker Lake settlement that the new impact of a
profitable art market came to the Caribou Eskimos.

Art came suddenly in 1960, when Mrs Edith
Dodds, wife of a Northern Service Officer stationed
among them at Baker Lake, thought that it would be
a helpful thing to start a handicrafts class for the
Eskimo women in the lonely and disheartened group.
After a while she met James Houston who had
stimulated Eskimo art as a source of income among
the people of Cape Dorset on Baffin Island. He was
interested and was given two drawings by one of the
Eskimo women, a widow named Una. They were so
good that they were sent to go with an exhibition of
Cape Dorset art.

In the next year, the Dodds were sent to a station
in Ungava Bay where they met Bill Larmour, a Crafts
Development Officer from Ottawa. He was persuaded
to visit the lonely people at Baker Lake. He found a
beautiful carving had been made by an old hunter,
Angosaglo, and that decided his line. A wooden
house was erected as a centre to which children and
grown ups were always welcome. They saw him
carving and were delighted. Some went home and
spread the news through their families. Then a young
man from the group returned to them more healthy
than he had been, but still terribly crippled through
poliomyelitis. The people were grateful that Willie,
a junior kinsman of Angosaglo, was kindly treated
and brought to live among them. To show their
pleasure they brought carvings they had made.
A council of the people met, and it was again old
Angosaglo who suggested that he and some of the
other elders should show the youngsters how carvings
in ivory and stone were made in the old days.

The great interest aroused led to a steadily
advancing style of art. Things went so well that a
permanently resident Arts Officer was appointed,
Gabriel Gély, who taught people how to draw, to carve
in ivory and to make jewellery from the translucent
horn of caribou hooves. They were encouraged to
work at their own speed and depict their own subjects.
The work was a tremendous success. It sold and
brought cash which could be exchanged for goods.
Eskimos who would have starved now earned up to a
hundred dollars a month. Artists developed among
the craftsmen, and eventually some fine sculpture and
prints were produced which fetched good prices. The

79 Two whale bone masks. Possibly Alaskan, early 20th century.
(Gimpel Collection)

70

80

Caribou Eskimos had survived, and had escaped the heart-searching miseries of pauperism by producing work of their own which could help them earn a living in the modern world. It was all to the good that they went naturally to depict the living creatures of their world, including, of course, the caribou. So in modern times a tribe of hunters who had been lost in the terrible confusions of a changing world have found a new footing which promises to be a stepping off point to a more secure future.

We have mentioned the artists of Baffin Island. They have an important place in the story of modern Eskimo art. They have been people of active interests. For much more than a century they have been in contact with Europeans. Their original life-style has gradually changed, mostly under the influence of exchange of goods with the visiting whaler crews. There was rarely any shortage of food among them, and their initiative was shown by their journey in the 1860s to visit the Polar Eskimos when

81

82

they showed them traditions which had been lost in the centuries under the arctic night.

The impulse to a closer unity of the people came from the establishment of a school in about 1950. It was comparatively easy for the Canadian Government to plan for Eskimo development in this area. There was already good contact through the Hudson's Bay Company trading post at Cape Dorset which was set up in 1918. The new school among an Eskimo population already mostly Christian and used to meeting together caused some migration from outlying settlements because the Eskimo family is very closely integrated and people felt it was good to move near to the children. The result was a concentration of people around Cape Dorset in the

extreme south of the island. The community was already well off by Eskimo standards and their economy was based on the great wealth of the region in fur-bearing animals and fishing. The burden of the change fell mostly on the men who travelled further from home to reach the hunting and trapping areas. Trade was well established, and the Eskimos had a council which threw up an active leader who was

80 **Family** by Angosaglo and Tatunak and Toweener. Baker Lake, N.W.T., 1972.
81 **Four women** by Parr. Copper engraving (25 × 30 cm). Cape Dorset, N.W.T., 1963.
82 **Two sleeping families** by Sheeookjuk. A moss wick lamp stands beside them. Grey stone and ivory (5 × 16 × 16 cm). Cape Dorset, N.W.T., 1953. (Canadian Guild of Crafts – Quebec Branch, Montreal)

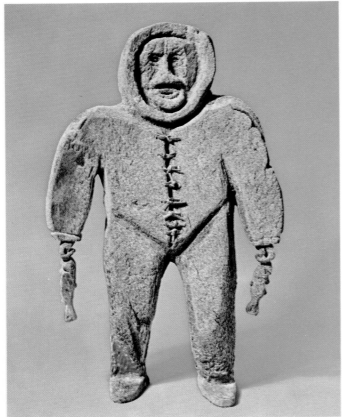

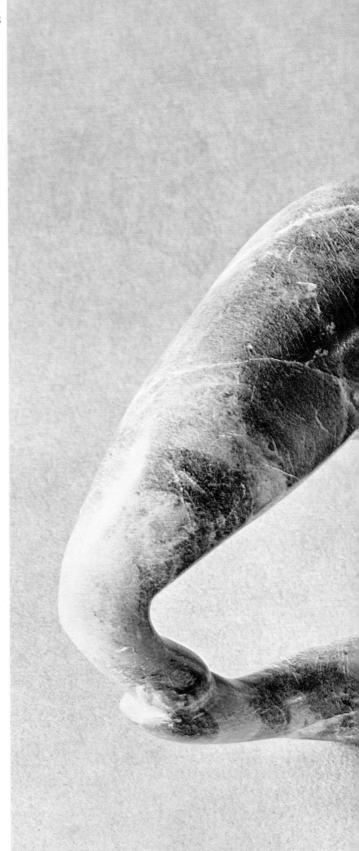

83 Man carrying two fish by Peterosee Anigliak. Whale bone
    (45 × 26 × 10.5 cm). Pangnirtung, N.W.T., about 1966.
    (Collection: Macmillan–Bloedel Limited, Vancouver, B.C.)
84 Owl by Qirluaq. Notable for the abstraction of the form.
    Grey-green mottled stone (15.5 × 12.5 × 7.3 cm). Repulse Bay,
    N.W.T., about 1968. (Collection: W. Eccles, Toronto)
85 Bear on ice by Manno. The bear looks at his reflection in the
    melting ice. Light grey-green stone (9 × 17 × 8.5 cm). Cape Dorset,
    N.W.T., 1964. (Collection: W. Eccles, Toronto)

86 Resting caribou by Oshooweetook 'B'. Green stone and bone (37 × 44 × 29 cm). Cape Dorset, N.W.T., 1970. (National Museum of Man, Ottawa)

87 Untitled stone cut by Parr. (76.5 × 65 cm). Probably representing geese or swans swimming. Cape Dorset, N.W.T., 1961.

instrumental in arranging for a church to be built. Thus when the art movement began to get under way there was a nucleus of a small township at Cape Dorset, almost as entirely assimilated into a new mixed culture as the little towns in Greenland.

In 1951 the Canadian Government sent James Houston to Cape Dorset with the avowed purpose of encouraging the local population to produce carvings and paintings for trade. There was considerable interest and several artists were happy at the chance of turning their abilities into an additional means of providing for their families. In this case there was no abandonment of Eskimo life since trapping and

hunting were so important economically that when the hunting seasons arrived the artists simply went away to the icefields. The women, however, had much less work to do. Improved economics meant that they had a cash income and that in turn fitted out the families in woollen clothes imported for use during the warmer months of the year. The superior ancient style of fur clothing was retained for use during the colder weather. Thus women of Cape Dorset have had leisure to employ their skills in making art of importance. Some of them became the makers of the first arctic lithographic prints from stone. They had learned from the white teachers and

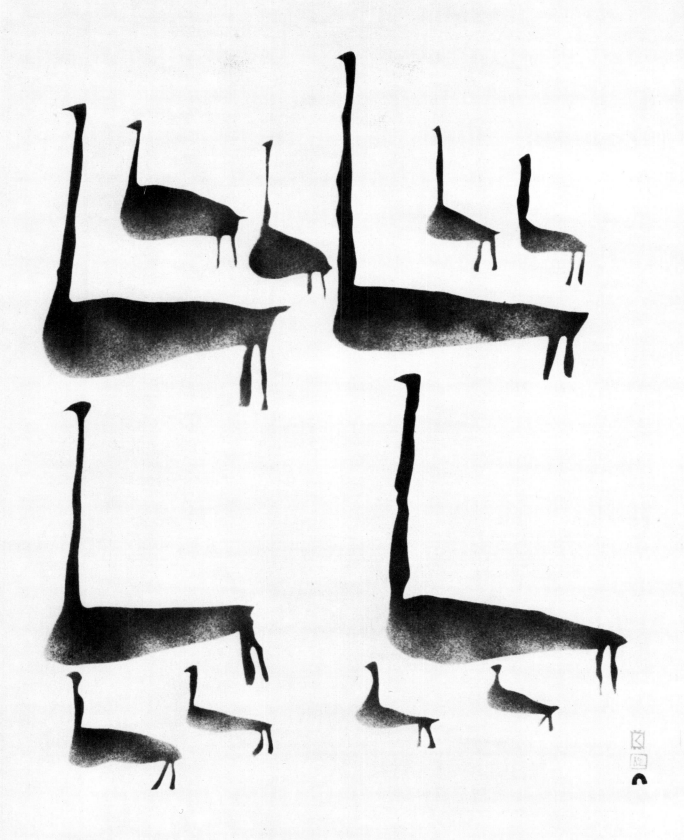

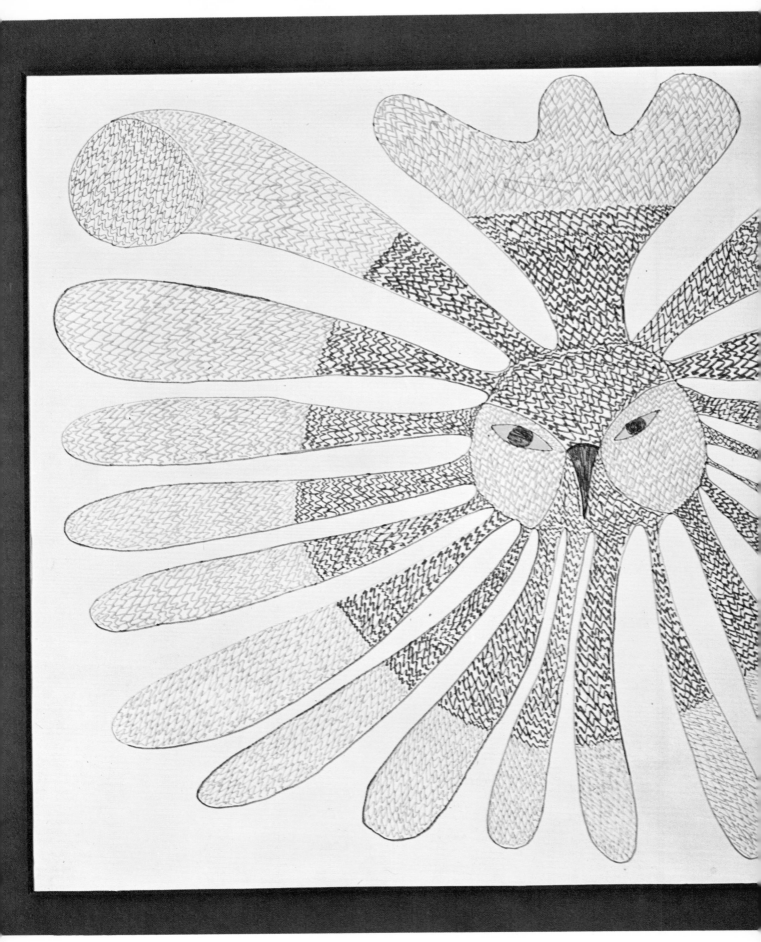

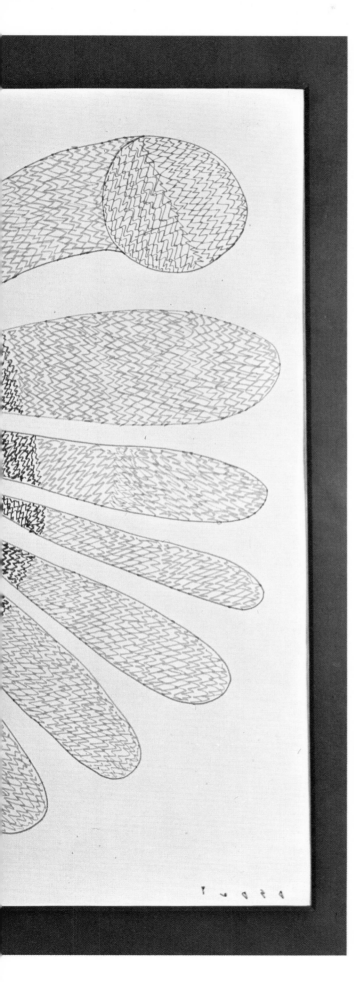

acquired a technique, but their subjects were the life of their own people in the setting of the living world of arctic Canada. It was with this background of artistic development among an advanced Eskimo community that James Houston went to the Caribou Eskimos and found them similarly responsive.

The art of Cape Dorset has importance for all of the sixty or seventy families permanently settled there. It is part of a general economic development of trade combined with cottage industry. The Eskimos have shown great acumen in organising this new life. They were given some state encouragement and have formed their own West Baffin Eskimo Co-operative, which supplied not only art but also beautiful skin garments and ivory and stone jewellery. Eventually they have been able to establish a shop of their own in friendly rivalry with the Hudson's Bay Company.

Today the Eskimos of Cape Dorset live in framed wooden houses with double walls, dry and easily heated in winter. In the summer they hunt from canvas tents. In many households the dog sledge has been replaced by the petrol-driven skidoo. Electricity is available, but the climate has prevented the installation of piped water. People have radios, watch television and provide enough material for a monthly aeroplane service to be maintained. A new form of Eskimo culture is developing in which the people preserve their identity while making use of the advantages, particularly in trade, which come from the mechanised civilisation of the modern world. Further steps will be taken, probably in the direction of animal farming over the vast spaces available on Baffin Island.

The development of arts reached the lonely Copper Eskimos on Victoria Island and around the mouth of the Coppermine River rather late. Like the other peoples of the arctic shores they had a long contact with the sailors on the whaling ships. They had met ethnologists who were interested in their use of raw copper for tools. They were much admired for their skill in blending furs for dress. But the hard fact was that apart from the losses from respiratory illnesses they were finding that the returns from hunting were continually decreasing and that it was desirable to move nearer to the settlement of Holman on the west coast of Victoria Island. Kalvak, an Eskimo widow in her sixties, when asked to make a skin parka for the Oblate missionary, Father Tardy, picked up a pencil from his desk and made a rough drawing of the design. At many later meetings Kalvak gave long accounts of the folklore of the Copper Eskimos. She had this knowledge through her husband who had

88 Owl by Kenojuak. Drawing. Cape Dorset, N.W.T., mid 20th century. (Gimpel Collection)

been a famous and powerful angakoq. As she told the stories she developed a talent for graphic art, making illustrations, sometimes on paper and sometimes as cut-outs in skin. Her enthusiasm brought four other artists in the Holman settlement to the missionary. They all produced interesting work of gradually increasing freedom, and in their own style. They had no direct art education at all but expressed their ideas directly in stark black on white, often in cut-out silhouettes.

It was as late as 1961 that Father Tardy saw Eskimo art, a Cape Dorset print hanging in the hospital at Yellowknife. He enquired about the process and when he returned to Holman he got two or three of the older boys to try out screen prints from blocks made of sealskin. The work was not too interesting, mostly because the boys needed to spend as much time as possible hunting. But during the slack season of winter, some of the older hunters proved more willing to spend time making blocks and printing from them. It was important that two of the first batch of prints sold at five dollars apiece. However there was little further success until in 1963 when the Department of Northern Affairs and National Resources sent out Barry Comber of the Toronto College of Art to guide the Holman artists. They were somewhat reluctant to start again, but enjoyed being given freedom to draw whatever they wished. Then they began to sell again. In 1964 a local deposit of fine-grained limestone was found. The skin blocks were discarded and lithographic inks were used on the stone enabling editions of up to twenty copies to be produced. The new process was very successful, and much more colour was possible in the products. Here Kalvak came in again. Unable to handle the limestone blocks which were too heavy for her, she produced designs on paper which were transferred to stone by the other members of the group. In 1965 a series of prints was sent to the Eskimo Art Committee who approved most of them for sale, and at an exhibition in St. John, New Brunswick, the Holman prints sold out. Once more art had become a source of added income to a remote Eskimo group. An especially interesting feature of Eskimo lithographs is the emphasis on soft and deep colours, particularly blue and red. This is very close to the use of ink colouring in bone engravings from Siberian Eskimos, and it may be that the choice reflects facets of arctic life and belongs particularly to Eskimo tradition.

The most easterly area for the production of Eskimo art is at Killinek (Cape Chidley), where Ungava Bay meets the Torngak Mountains beside the Davis Strait. The region was rich in sea foods, but the Eskimo settlement there was few in numbers; in 1952 there were only thirty-two individuals. Their livelihood was restricted because their best boat could not be repaired and there were not enough young men among them to undertake the hard work of the food quest. They were given government assistance and a fishery and canning station were established. School was attended, and the community prospered so that outlying groups of hunters came in. Among the new work prepared were engravings, stone sculpture from the many beautiful stones obtainable on the rocky coast, and ivory carving. In the slowly growing community where shortage of human power almost brought the settlement to extinction, there has been an acceptance of help and a deliberate choice of a new way of living. In this the production of art has played a minor part, but it has had a good effect on the personal lives of the people, who have discovered the pleasures of individual skills once again. Of course in an area of rich sea resources the artists remain a minority, but they prove that the Eskimo is by nature able to express life in terms of graphic art. And works of art form part of the material traded through the local Eskimo co-operative.

The development of modern art among the Eskimo people dates apparently from about 1948 when James Houston brought a steatite carving from an artist at Povungnituk on the coast of Hudson Bay. In this region the local people had worked in the beautiful local stones of serpentine and steatite, easy to work and giving beautiful surfaces if finished with care. The art had, even at that early phase, become accepted by the local people as worthwhile. It is from this contact that the steady growth of Canadian Government help to the artists in Eskimo communities can be dated. The idea has spread. The white teachers have in general avoided teaching more than technique, and the styles and the meanings of the new art remain truly Eskimo. They differ widely among themselves, each individual having a style which is usually reflected by the local community. But each community has its own ways and is not often influenced by the art of other Eskimo groups.

However, the idea of art being distinct from everyday craftsmanship is a new one to the Eskimos. It has been hard to abandon the old ways, particularly since the break-down of the old way of living has been due to the disappearance of caribou and whale as well as many other animals. Hardship and hunger have been hard spurs to change. The love of children and family unity have been the silken cords which have drawn the Eskimos into a new life. Over the whole arctic the numbers of Eskimos are steadily increasing again, while the number of settlements has decreased. They are able to live in greater contact with their fellows, which after all is a satisfaction for the Eskimo genius for friendship. In these

surroundings there has been a practical attempt by the Eskimos to assimilate in their own way. They have been fortunate in finding friends among administrators and teachers who did not impose white standards upon them without consultation. For the white man, too, the world has changed and the ideas of a century ago have been broken down, so that Eskimos are now seen as adult and intelligent people and not as perpetual childish wards in need of care and assistance.

On the extreme boundaries of the Eskimos, the people are full citizens of the countries which have control of their geographical regions. The U.S.S.R. has assimilated the few Siberian Eskimos of the Bering Strait. Denmark has given full and free citizenship to the Greenlanders. The U.S.A. and Canada still have a protective organisation to look after Eskimo affairs, but in practice the Eskimos have a share in discussing and organising future activities. This freedom and democratisation is steadily growing. With it an art market has developed, in a loosely organised way in Denmark and the U.S.A., and in a much more closely organised fashion in Canada. But in all areas Eskimo co-operative trading centres

are organised and active. They seem to be the natural way for the Eskimos to organise themselves. They have always been at once interdependent within the community though self-reliant as individuals. They have rejected dictation even within the village, but have listened with respect to the wise elders of the community. So the primitive Eskimo codes of social life are still powerful forces in the modern world.

The production is not a matter of group working on a time chain, but of free creation and free trading through the local organisation. For Eskimo art a new world is opening. But how does it look to us on the receiving end of the market?

89 **The land of ice and snow** by Kalvak. The Eskimo family are building their igloo while the sun lady and the moon man are still visible in the sky. Print. Holman, N.W.T., 1970.

Eskimo Art and Artists

When people come across traditional Eskimo art in museums there is usually a friendly fascination. The little figures of animals and people polished in bone and ivory have a great charm about them. They reflect a peaceful life in a world of hardship and beauty. Emotional responses towards the little animals are conditioned by the type of our civilisation; they are not usually seen as the quarries of the hunter but as the pets of childhood. Even the terrible polar bear becomes a cuddly creature seen at the zoo. The tendency to show the human figure naked and in a static verticality does include some deep level linkage with sex, but overt sexuality is rare, not because Eskimo artists lacked erotic interest, but because they had no need to stress it in a life which was natural and fulfilling. Our conscious reaction to Eskimo sculpture is an appreciation of the surface forms. There is an element of pleasure in handling the ivories. These carvings were meant to be handled, oiled and fondled. To touch them is to enjoy a tactile pleasure important to the understanding of their meaning. Whether we can judge their artistic quality separately from their own cultural setting is not in question. The majority of works, especially of the Thule phase of Eskimo culture, can be immediately understood as works of art. Questions of proportion, rhythmic structure, and unity of appearance from all angles are quite proper in appreciating them. They can be compared with small animal forms of Western cultures such as Roman or Renaissance bronzes. They have a different degree of realism largely because of the limitation of means available to the old time Eskimos, but they stand the comparison well, and to many people the Eskimo works are superior because of the artist's natural understanding of animal forms which is distinct from the intellectual understanding of the European artist. Therein lies the importance of small Eskimo sculpture: its simplicity of approach.

How can we judge Eskimo art through the time scale which is only recently becoming apparent? We have seen so many different styles, from the art of the earliest peoples of Alaska and Siberia who decorated roughly shaped ivory carvings with delicate linear patterns, to the vigorous and magical sculptures of the Dorset culture and the more delicate and elegant products of the Thule culture. Critics differ sharply in their assessment of the aesthetic quality of Eskimo art, yet it is a subjective criticism because we have little reliable knowledge of the meaning and purpose of many of the pieces. All we know is that since early times there was a great emphasis on the angakoq and his religious trance phenomena. The famous ivory mask-frames worn around the face of an angakoq belong to the early Ipiutak people who lived near Point Hope in Alaska. Dorset culture artists produced sculptures of seals and polar bears; the bear sometimes had human limbs and we are sure it is an angakoq in disguise. Likewise the Igloolik wooden masks with characteristic flaring nostrils, and the comb with the demon face all had a magical significance. It is not until contact occurred with outsiders that Eskimo art developed the features of sailor-inspired scrimshaw.

We also know that many items of everyday use were carved or decorated with good luck symbols. Such charms might be made by any member of the community, not necessarily the angakoq. They were, however, magical and their intention was often successful in their position of a psychological support to the hunter. The making of the carving put the artist in contact with the soul of the animal, or perhaps one should say 'idea' in the Greek sense. When using the arrow the marksman looked for success. There was less hesitation and doubt about the shot, and so it was in fact likely to be more successful. Naturally such magic works best for people who are living in the untroubled world of the unconscious mind without the considered need to rationalise every act into a conscious movement for a conscious purpose. It is because of this unthinking production of the old ivory carvings that they so often appeal directly to us. We rationalise, 'this is a bear, that a seal', but somehow that animal seems more attractive than just a representation. It has something of the animal itself. The unconscious mind responds by a kind of reflection of the original idea, not complete of course, because our material culture is so different, but the animal becomes much more of a real experience than

90 **Mother and child with a fish.** Green stone and ivory (17 × 11 × 8 cm). Port Harrison, Quebec, 1954–1955. (Collection: Mr and Mrs John K.B. Robertson, Ottawa)

91 **Swan and duck.** Green stone. From the Canadian arctic, 20th century. (Gimpel Collection)

92 **Bird with wings spread** by Sheeookjuk. Green stone ($12 \times 24 \times 5$ cm). Cape Dorset, N.W.T., about 1960. (Collection: Mr and Mrs John K.B. Robertson, Ottawa)
93 **Bear.** Serpentine. From the Canadian arctic, 20th century. (Gimpel Collection)

91

the simple fact of a carved ivory representation would warrant.

Many of the Eskimo works of art of the nineteenth century became known through the sailors on whalers and fishermen from the fleets sailing to Alaska and Greenland. They included many a pleasant trinket, a bunch of carved fish, a carving of a hunter with his dog team, or indeed any other representation of arctic life. Sometimes sailors picked up little gambling sets of miniature birds and mammals. They were charming, and amused the people at home who had no conception of their serious purpose as gambling counters. Naturally, not many of the charms and magical material of the angakoq found their way to the south. They were rather frightening objects, and when the people became Christians they hid or destroyed many of the sacred objects of the old days. Those which reached southern lands were collected by ethnologists, acquired from sympathetic

friendship and payment in kind or cash. Although we shall probably never know the exact traditions behind the prehistoric objects, they form a link with the folklore which is enshrined in modern Eskimo art.

Much of Eskimo art shows an interpretation of folklore in connection with the heavenly bodies. The sun is a beautiful lady with tattooed face, and the moon is an impulsive young hunter. The Pleiades are the hunter and his dogs who chased the white bear up into the sky. The Aurora Borealis is the world of souls who suffered sudden death in this life, who now sometimes come out to play football with a walrus skull across the sky. Whether Eskimo technicians and engineers of the future will laugh at the old fantasy world is unclear, but to judge by what has happened in our own culture, there will always be people who tell the old stories and feel in their hearts that there is an ancient truth preserved in them even though it is expressed in a most unscientific way.

Eskimo folklore includes some quite charming stories which can still have a reference to art. Here is one about a rock by the sea shore. Once upon a time there was a poor woman; she had no relatives and no friends. People gave her scraps of food and bits of skin if she worked for them; sometimes they grew angry with her and abused her. She was unhappy and friendless. One day when she was rowing a umiak she gradually grew more and more tired. So she rowed to the shore and sat on a rock with her head on her hands thinking sadly of the cruelty of people and her own hopeless situation. She wished she could die and that her hard labour and thankless tasks were all finished. Then it came into her mind that it would be lovely to become a rock like the one she was sitting on. Then she would always be resting and see all the sea and sky without any more pain. She wished so strongly that her wish was heard. A crow came cawing down from the sky; he circled around her three times, and

cawed and cawed, and as he cawed she slowly turned into a rock without losing her shape. Then afterwards when the sea hunters went by her rock some of them would make little gifts of needles, blubber or tobacco, and some women passing by in their boat were touched by her sad story and put a beautiful necklace around her neck. But now the sea animals have gone away and so have the Eskimos and the stone woman is once again left all alone.

There are many tales of sadness; perhaps they were told to children so that when they grew up they would be merciful. They belong to the world whence

---

94 **Composition of tree with owl** by Josephee Kakee. Whale bone and ivory (66 × 81 × 26 cm). Pangnirtung, N.W.T., 1968. (National Museum of Man, Ottawa)

95 **The Migration** by Joe Talirunili. Grey stone, bone and skin (33 × 32 × 19 cm). Povungnituk, Quebec, 1964. (Collection: Pat Furneaux, North Augusta, Ontario)

Little Red Riding Hood and Hansel and Gretel came into the European stories. There were also the giants. Not all giants were human either. There was a time long ago when a great shaman was taken by the torngak (a spirit guide and protector) to see a marvel he had always wished to behold. Every year since he was a child he had seen the caribou come from the north and pass south in great herds, crossing rivers and ever seeking their way to some distant goal. 'Where do the caribou go in the winter?' was his constant request to the spirits who came to his séances. Now he was to be shown the way, but first the torngak warned him that he must never tell other people where he had been. He promised, and then the torngak told him the direction in which to seek. He gave the hunter two pairs of magic boots. Then the search went on. For two moons the hunter-shaman walked over the tundra. Patiently he trudged ever forward, until the torngak appeared again. He was told to stop and be silent until sundown. Only one more thing must he do and that was to avoid wishing to kill anything he saw. He vowed to suppress his natural desires as a hunter and so was allowed to remain.

As the sun set the world was bathed in a shimmering light of magic; he moved a little and then saw afar off an enormous house of rocks and moss. It was entered by a huge tunnel before which stood a bull moose with spreading antlers. The animal was so huge that he was terrified, especially when he realised that the mists swirling towards it were vast herds of caribou from all directions. Silently they walked towards the great Master of the Caribou. They walked under his body without touching him and went to find warmth and food and rest in the great house under the earth. When all the caribou were home for the winter the giant lay down and rested, guarding the cave until the time should come when the herds must return northwards with the summer.

Then the torngak came again to the hunter-shaman. He gave him wings and he flew through the mists to find himself back again among the well-known rocks on the shore near his house. There the shaman was welcomed by the people for he had been away a long time, and they wished to hear his stories again. But now he had a new tale to tell of the giant caribou, though never did he divulge the exact locality where the giant caribou guarded the cave where the animals sheltered through the winter.

In modern times less caribou come every year, and yet however widely the hunters search for the mysterious home of the animals they can never find it.

96 Mythological hare-dog-seal and ptarmigan by Peter Pitseolak. Drawing. From the Canadian arctic, 20th century. (Gimpel Collection)

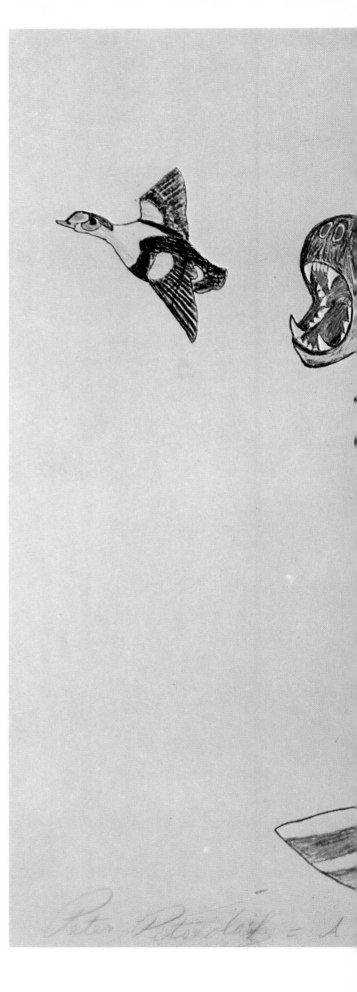

So they have to seek for other means of living.

There are other little tales which explain natural things. Ravens are black because once upon a time there was a great feast, and the food was cooking on a fire of wood. The raven quarrelled with the owl who was giving the feast and the owl was so angry that he picked up the black charred wood and threw it all over raven so that he became black and never was clean again. The seagull and the raven challenged each other to a race to decide who would have most children. They set off round the course but the seagull was much more tricky than the raven and went around a shorter flight much more often. In the end the seagull won, and that is why white children, like the seagull, grew up into white people and took all the land for themselves. Which is rather an unkind story but also somewhat true.

The subject of folk tales occurs strongly in modern Eskimo graphics. In some cases drawings depict tales of the hunter and the intelligent bears; others tell of the use of magical charms which become dangerous. There are pictures of daily life and animals too. In many cases the details of the drawing are richly filled with stippling or hachures which give the effect of fur. Some drawings of women display the old favourite tattoo marks. In other cases the figures in the picture are black silhouettes with a few white lines to add details. These works are often stencils, cut from thin sheets of skin. They also appear as block prints made with hide printing blocks. The use of leather for blocks has some advantages in a certain softness of texture, and sometimes of a very slight surface patterning.

This printing from leather is a new art form which derived originally from skin outline figures exactly cut out and stitched as a kind of fur appliqué on seal or caribou skins. This is used nowadays for ornamental garments, and for fur mats and wall hangings. It is naturally an art form made by women, because in the past a woman's life was linked closely with the home, where she spent much of her time making beautiful fur garments from the skins brought home by father as clothing for the family. In the old times this work was done outdoors in the summer, and on calm days the seamstress was often dressed only in her boots so that the sun should bring pleasure to her naked body. Alas, as some Eskimo pictures show, the ladies too often became the victims of ravenous mosquitoes.

The minuscule art of old times was worked in ivory, often engraved, and in local stones: slate, steatite and serpentine. Nothing was large; a walrus tusk was quite the largest surface to be carved. Most of the product was very personal and private because it contained individual magic brought from within

by the artist. But now that there are international markets and a real demand for high quality work a larger variety of size occurs. Boulders of the right stone are sought out, and often they are found most easily by prospecting the coast for stones of about the right size. The surface quality and colour of the stone is most easily seen below water and many artists go with friends on prospecting journeys to find stones to bring back on the sledge to work at in the local trading co-operative workshop. Another source of attractive material is the ancient house ruins found here and there which were made by the Tornrit of the Dorset culture. Here are whale ribs and great vertebrae as well as the occasional massive walrus skull. The old bone is usually weathered to a dull surface of light grey, and in most cases the cancellar tissue is exposed to give a most attractive surface, though not a pleasant one to handle. However, these natural forms belonging to the Eskimo past seem to suggest ideas to the artist, so that in this material many

strange spirit beings take form, and menacingly emerge from their long sleep in the unconscious heart of the people. Sometimes a frightening torngak will emerge. He is a spirit at once human and animal, but never truly human; his mind is turned to mischief and trickery so he is grotesque and menacing. His happiness is to cause trouble, to wreck a kayak, to make a whale destroy its hunter, to cause the ice floe to crack and drown people, or to start sudden storms. The torngak is not pleasant, but he is an expression of the real uncertainties of life in the arctic; he is the archetypal trickster seen as many beings of ambivalent character. However the same artist who will make a torngak one day will at another time use a similar block of material to make an Eskimo hunter trudging home with a captured seal behind him, or a fine fox on his back.

Many modern works of Eskimo art have been made in the haven of Christian missions, but they are rarely on Christian themes. They also tend to show Eskimo life in one aspect or another. If a biblical story is incorporated in a carving it is put very properly in Eskimo terms. An Eskimo interpretation of the calming of the tempest on the lake, the miracle of the loaves and fishes, or the resurrection of Lazarus may seem strange to the white man, but they are all the more real to the artists when the story is stated in terms of Eskimo life and not copied from a nineteenth-century Bible picture. Nevertheless, we can expect to find more expressions about animals and family life than anything else. The surrounding of deep affection is very clearly felt. The family in its thick furs, clustered altogether in companionable unity, is as common as the mother with the child nestling in her hood, put there for warmth and cuddly comfort. Similarly, even the quarries of the hunter are shown as living, sentient beings, regarded with that

97 Skeletal tupilak with human feet and spirit faces in its shoulders. Wood (15.4 cm long). From Angmagssalik, Greenland, about 1900. (Danish National Museum, Copenhagen)

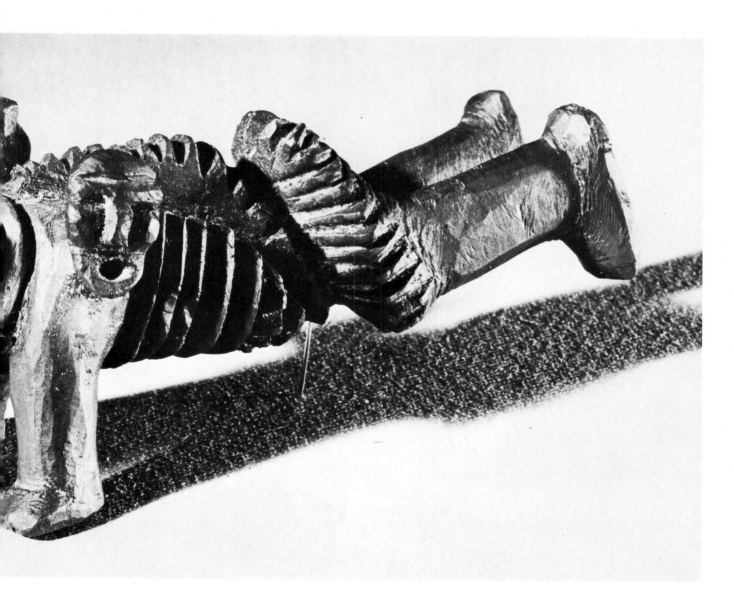

98

understanding which marks true affection. Because that traditional Eskimo life has never totally disappeared, the spiritual link between human and animal has never been quite broken.

The products of modern Eskimo artists remain based in the life of the Eskimo people. An artist may make use of a traditional idea, and yet say something fresh in a new medium. It may be that the critic can see only the animal or the pattern as something graceful and well executed, but the artist can see an expression of local life, or an ancient folk tale or even an actual historical event. A scene of a crowded whale-boat carved in steatite, records a famous migration in search of food which took place in about 1912. The artist remembered the names of many of the people involved.

The simple music of the Eskimos, with its traditional songs and dances to the thunderous music of the huge tambourine-like drums, is now replaced by tapes played on a transistorised recorder. But the festivals held at traditional times, the old days for starting sea hunting or for returning to the land, persist and old songs mix with modern whenever a drum dance can be arranged. There is a descent from the past, but it is partial and the old atmosphere of magic has gone; yet the occasions are ones in which a skilled dancer can give an acrobatic performance and a juggler mystify the audience much as he might have in ancient times. On such occasions people are happy and free to talk and sing as a community. Here hopes are discussed and sorrows condoled. The Eskimo community sense has not diminished, and, while

98 Wall hanging by Naomi Ityi showing scenes from Eskimo folklore. Appliqué on wool (71.5 × 107 cm). Baker Lake, N.W.T., 1971.
99 Wall hanging by Irene Avaalaqiaq. Appliqué on wool (132.5 × 142.5 cm). Baker Lake, N.W.T., 1971.

99

dancing and music are arts in themselves, they also provide material for the visual arts either in sculpture or graphics.

But beyond the festivities and the new economic life the vastness of the arctic still enfolds the Eskimos. They do not wish to desert their land; it is in some ways a parental home for all of them, and its dangerous beauty is a matter of deep affection among them. Even in the most advanced groups there are times when the people prefer to go out in their summer tents to hunt and fish in something like the old way, or at least the way of their grandparents. Boys still play at hunting and know many stories of the adventures of the old time hunters. For three thousand years the Eskimos have endured the rigours of arctic life. Their art, even at its simplest, stands for their

indomitable courage and capability in the face of adversity. Yet today the whole rhythm of arctic life is threatened by an enemy more terrible than nature. Supplies of game have steadily decreased, the ocean is overfished, the whale, the polar bear, the walrus and the musk ox are all in danger of extinction. And the curse of pollution has fallen in these remote lands. The struggle for survival continues, but now man is the enemy. The Inuit, the 'people', have much to teach us when it comes to the condition and behaviour of man. Hopefully, through their art, they will succeed and will survive as themselves in the modern preliminary to the Aquarian age.

100 Flour scoop made from extinct mammoth ivory with scenes of fox trapping and other animals. (Collection: Hudson's Bay Company)

Index

Numbers in **bold** type refer to illustrations

Some further reading

Bandi, H.G., **Urgeschichte der Eskimo**. Stuttgart, 1965

Birkett-Smith, K., many books, but general work is **The Eskimos**. Copenhagen and London, 1936

Burland, C.A., **Men Without Machines**. London, 1967

Caillois, R., **Chefs d'œuvre des arts Indiens et Esquimaux du Canada**. Paris, 1969

Canadian Department of Northern Affairs and National Resources, **Canadian Eskimo Art**. Ottawa, 1956

Canadian Eskimo Arts Council, **Sculpture of the Inuit: masterworks of the Canadian Arctic**, exhibition catalogue. Canada, 1971

Carpenter, E., **Eskimo**. Oxford and Toronto, 1959

Collins, H.B., 'Prehistoric Art of the Alaskan Eskimo', **Smithsonian Miscellaneous Collections**, Vol. 81 no. 14. Washington 1937; 'Archaeology of St. Lawrence Island, Alaska', **Smithsonian Miscellaneous Collections**, Vol. 96 no. 1. Washington, 1937

Danish Anthropological Society, **Folk**, periodical. Copenhagen, 1964 ff.

Dockstader, F.J., **Indian Art of North America**. Greenwich, Connecticut, 1966

Haberland, W., **North America** (Art of the World). Baden Baden 1964, London 1968

Himmelheber, H., **Eskimokünstler**. Eisenach, 1953

Hoffman, J., **The Graphic Art of the Eskimos**, U.S. National Museum Report for 1899, pp 739–968

Holtved, E., **Eskimo Art**. 1947

Hudson's Bay Company, 'Eskimo Art', **The Beaver**, autumn issue 1967. Winnipeg

Jenness, D., various **Reports of the Canadian Arctic Expeditions**. Department of Mines, Ottawa

Judson, K.B., **Myths and Legends of Alaska**. Chicago, 1911

Larmour, W.T., **Inunnit: The Art of the Canadian Eskimo** (in English and French). Ottawa, 1967

Larsen, H., and Rainey F., 'Ipiutak and the Arctic Whale-Hunting Cultures'. **American Museum of Natural History, Anthropological Papers**, Vol. 42. New York, 1948

Martijn, C., 'Canadian Eskimo Carvings in Historical Perspective', **Anthropos**, Vol. LIX. Fribourg, 1965

Meldgaard, J., **Eskimo Sculpture**. London, 1960

Rasmussen, K., **Across Arctic America**

Ray, D.J., **Artists of the Tundra and the Sea**. Seattle, 1961; **Eskimo Masks, Art and Ceremony**. Seattle and London, 1967

Swinton, G., **Eskimo Sculpture**. Toronto, 1965

Thule: (various authors) **Reports of the Fifth Thule Expedition, 1921–1924**, in 10 volumes. Copenhagen, 1927–1952

Williamson, R., 'The Spirit of Keewatin', **The Beaver**, summer issue, 1967. Winnipeg

Acknowledgments

The museums, galleries and private collectors listed in the captions demonstrate the generous help we have received from many friends around the world. In particular we are grateful to the late Charles Gimpel for permission to photograph so many beautiful things from his private collection, to the Canadian Eskimo Arts Council for permission to photograph their exhibition during its short stay in London, and to the Hudson's Bay Company who allowed us to photograph their collections just before they returned to Canada. The British Museum, in its special section, The Museum of Mankind, has also given us considerable help in allowing us to take photographs at very short notice. From everyone whom we have asked for assistance in illustrating this book we have received unstinting help. We only hope that their generosity finds some small reward in the use we have made of their material in these pages.

Sources of photographs

American Museum of Natural History, New York 8, 56; Anthropological Museum, University of Aberdeen 68; K. J. Butler, Winnipeg, Manitoba 98, 99; Canadian Eskimo Arts Council, Ottawa, Ontario 2, 3, 10, 14, 27, 37, 44, 72, 82, 86, 89, 90, 94, 95; Cincinnati Art Museum, Cincinnati, Ohio 38; City of Liverpool Museums 46; Danish National Museum, Copenhagen 75; Hamlyn Group–Hawkley Studio Associates 5, 15, 16, 17, 18, 21, 23, 25, 30, 31, 32, 40, 42, 47, 48, 54, 55, 58, 59, 60, 65, 67, 69, 70, 71, 76, 79, 83, 84, 85, 88, 91, 92, 93, 96, 100; Hamlyn Group Picture Library 19, 26, 29, 34, 35, 41, 50, 52; Jørgen Meldgaard, Copenhagen 4, 6, 11, 12, 13, 39, 43, 73, 74, 97; Hugh M. Moss Ltd., London 1, 20, 28, 80, 81, 87; Museum of the American Indian, New York 22, 33, 53; Museum of Mankind, London 36, 49, 51, 57, 63, 64; Museum of Primitive Art, New York 9, Royal Scottish Museum, Edinburgh 61, 62, 66; Smithsonian Institution, Museum of Natural History, Washington, D.C. 24; University of Alaska Museum, College, Alaska 7, 45, 77, 78.